URBAN HIKES
DENVER

A GUIDE TO DENVER'S GREATEST
URBAN HIKING ADVENTURES

NO LONGER PROPERTY OF
DENVER PUBLIC LIBRARY

Katie Hearsum

FALCONGUIDES

GUILFORD, CONNECTICUT

FALCONGUIDES®

An imprint of Globe Pequot, the trade division of
The Rowman & Littlefield Publishing Group, Inc.
4501 Forbes Blvd., Ste. 200
Lanham, MD 20706
www.rowman.com

Falcon and FalconGuides are registered trademarks and Make Adventure Your Story is a trademark of The Rowman & Littlefield Publishing Group, Inc.

Distributed by NATIONAL BOOK NETWORK

Copyright © 2022 The Rowman & Littlefield Publishing Group, Inc.
Photos by Katie Hearsum
Maps by Melissa Baker

All rights reserved. No part of this book may be reproduced in any form or by any electronic or mechanical means, including information storage and retrieval systems, without written permission from the publisher, except by a reviewer who may quote passages in a review.

British Library Cataloguing in Publication Information available

Library of Congress Cataloging-in-Publication Data

Names: Hearsum, Katie, author.
Title: Urban hikes Denver : a guide to the city's greatest urban hiking adventures / Katie Hearsum.
Description: Guilford, Connecticut : FalconGuides, 2022. | Includes index. | Summary: "A guide to over 80 miles of trails easily within reach from downtown Denver"— Provided by publisher.
Identifiers: LCCN 2021035815 (print) | LCCN 2021035816 (ebook) | ISBN 9781493059577 (paperback) | ISBN 9781493059584 (epub)
Subjects: LCSH: Hiking—Colorado—Denver Region—Guidebooks. | Trails—Colorado—Denver Region—Guidebooks. | Denver Region (Colo.)—Guidebooks.
Classification: LCC GV199.42.C62 D465 2022 (print) | LCC GV199.42.C62 (ebook) | DDC 796.5109788/83—dc23
LC record available at https://lccn.loc.gov/2021035815
LC ebook record available at https://lccn.loc.gov/2021035816

♾™ The paper used in this publication meets the minimum requirements of American National Standard for Information Sciences—Permanence of Paper for Printed Library Materials, ANSI/ NISO Z39.48-1992.

The author and The Rowman & Littlefield Publishing Group, Inc., assume no liability for accidents happening to, or injuries sustained by, readers who engage in the activities described in this book.

CONTENTS

Background photo: Barr Lake State Park's wildlife refuge trails feature several nice boardwalks offering lakefront access and prime wildlife viewing opportunities.

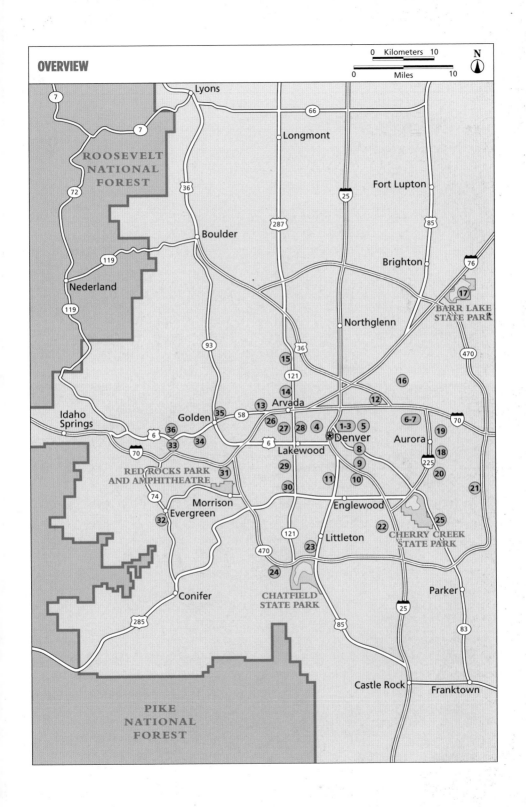

Some old-fashioned things like fresh air and sunshine are hard to beat.
—Laura Ingalls Wilder

Thanks to the relatively flat landscape and southwestern location of the city of Littleton, this route offers panoramic mountain views of the foothills.

MEET YOUR GUIDE

KATIE HEARSUM is a Colorado-based freelance journalist who has been covering topics relating to tourism and outdoor recreation for publications such as *U.S. News & World Report*, *Elevation Outdoors*, and *5280* (Denver's award-winning city magazine) for more than a decade.

An avid hiker and nature lover, she has trekked all over the world—along rocky cliffs on Italy's Amalfi coast, across glacial streams in Patagonia, and through swarms of mosquitoes in the Boundary Waters Canoe Area Wilderness. Still, her favorite trails are the ones found in her own backyard in Colorado.

Katie is a member of the Grand County Community of Writers and the Outdoor Writers Association of America, and is a community ambassador for the Continental Divide Trail Coalition. You can connect with Katie and read more of her work by visiting www.katiehearsum.com.

BEFORE YOU HIT THE TRAIL

The City of Denver manages one of the best networks of parks, trails, and open space in the country. In addition to offering about 80 miles of off-street trails within the city limits, it also has a unique collection of mountain parks comprising a whopping 14,000 acres of open space and conservation areas. From picturesque neighborhood paths to commuter routes to rugged trails, wherever you find yourself in Denver you can be sure there is a nice place nearby to take a hike, whether you're looking to fill a lunch break, a layover, or a leisurely afternoon.

DEFINING URBAN HIKES

What exactly constitutes a "hike"? Is it defined by a certain distance, elevation, or duration? Or a specific type of terrain or surface material? Home to fifty-eight mountain peaks soaring over 14,000 feet tall (known as "fourteeners"), an array of world-class ski resorts, and the third most visited national park in the country, Rocky Mountain National Park, named for one of North America's most rugged mountain ranges, Colorado can be an intimidating place to hike. Some people just aren't satisfied until they've lost a toenail or suffered altitude sickness trying to reach the summit of one of the state's record-holding peaks, or lugged a week's worth of supplies on their back while braving the elements to conquer a "thru-hike" such as the 3,100-mile Continental Divide National Scenic Trail.

But those folks would be missing out on the simple, satisfying experiences they can have closer to home: the cherry blossoms cascading along Cherry Creek, bald eagles soaring over Barr Lake, a stellar sunset in City Park—just to name a few. A few moments in nature can work wonders, like a salve for the soul, and are key to finding balance and peace in the modern world. This book will guide those seeking a taste of the great outdoors to such aforementioned experiences, without sacrificing creature comforts or making major investments of money, energy, and—most importantly—time.

Each of the trails detailed here was handpicked for its ease of access, quality and comfort of terrain, and the presence of conveniences such as water fountains, restrooms, sitting areas, and playgrounds. Many feature notable historic and cultural sites to pique the interest of both first-time visitors and longtime locals alike. And some are located near public transportation stations, offering easy access for all. These routes were selected with the perspective of flatlanders and families in mind, but even seasoned trekkers might discover a new trail to treasure in their daily lives—a new place to take the dog, fresh scenery for a daily jog, or maybe just a quiet spot to enjoy some solitude. The litany of health benefits that walking provides is astounding, and can be achieved in as little as just 10 minutes of movement. But, most importantly, it will help soothe the senses from too much screen time and give our minds something they crave: space to roam.

Enjoy panoramic views from Sloan Lake's elevated location.

URBAN HIKES FOR TRAVELERS

There are many ways to travel, but walking has always been my preferred way to explore a new place. In the age of high-speed and on-demand everything, adopting a slow travel mindset is more valuable than ever before. When first arriving in a new city, it's tempting to hop in a car and zip around town to the "must-see" landmarks and attractions. This mode of travel might be best if your goal is to simply cross things off your bucket list, but to truly get to know a place you must slow down and aim for quality over quantity. Walking teaches you to look for beauty in the mundane, which can often be more exciting to discover than the mainstream points of interest (though if you're hoping for the best of both worlds, don't miss the Downtown Landmarks Loop hike, custom-curated for travelers short on time). You'll find that this book is so much more than a trail guide—it also takes you on a tour of some of Denver's top neighborhoods, leading you to local-favorite restaurants, parks, and activities off the beaten tourist path.

WEATHER

Situated at 5,280 feet in elevation (hence the "Mile High" nickname), Denver is drenched with sunshine and blue skies most days, which can be a blessing and a curse for hikers. The strong sun paired with the high altitude can lead to severe dehydration and even altitude sickness, a flu-like ailment that commonly attacks people visiting from lower elevations. Always carry more water than you think you will need and wear sunscreen— even in the winter, and even on seemingly short, easy hikes.

Summers are generally hot and dry, with temperatures often soaring into the 90s. Summertime monsoons can deliver afternoon thunderstorms like clockwork, another blessing and curse for hikers. While these storms help cool things off, they are often reliably unpredictable, swooping in seemingly out of nowhere, and sometimes bringing severe lightning and hail with them. A good rule of thumb is to plan to be off the trails no later than 3 p.m., especially if you're hiking in the foothills.

Winters are fairly mild in the cities along the Front Range, which may come as a surprise to some. It's not uncommon to have a 60-degree day in January (or a 20-degree night in July). Even when there is snowfall, the sun helps it melt quickly, making urban trails accessible year-round. That said, it's a good idea to have a pair of microspikes handy

The Star K Ranch wetlands offer a change of scenery from the flat grasslands.

The trailside rose gardens in Wash Park were designed to resemble those at Mount Vernon, President George Washington's Virginia estate.

on icy days for better traction. Snowshoeing is also encouraged, and you can buy or rent equipment at many Denver-area outdoors stores, as well as the use of trekking poles. Don't let the cold temps or snowy skies stop you from a great day of Denver hiking.

Finally, one characteristic of Denver weather that can be a bit pesky is the drastic temperature swings you can experience over the course of several hours, or truly even just minute to minute, depending on the time of year. Locals know that there's no such thing as bad weather, just bad clothing, so always dress in layers.

FLORA AND FAUNA

Denver is uniquely situated as a gateway between the eastern plains and the western mountains. Contrary to what most people picture, the city itself is more representative of a prairie environment than an alpine one. To the north and east, seemingly desolate grasslands are teeming with wildlife and provide ideal habitat for foxes, coyotes, snakes, rabbits, and nesting raptors. Cottonwood and willow trees line the area's many creeks, offering a lush ecosystem for birdlife and waterfowl, while blue grama (the state's native grass), rabbitbrush, and cactus cluster near the trails.

Black bears, mountain lions, and elk are most active among the pine and aspen groves of the South and West Metro and Foothills regions, though sightings are uncommon. In the summer, watch out (or, rather, listen) for rattlesnakes, which like to stretch themselves across sunny paths and curl under rocks. These rocks make it difficult for most plants to thrive, save for coniferous trees like blue spruce, the Colorado state tree, and the lodgepole pines that sway in the mountain breeze. Those familiar with old cowboy songs will be delighted to discover that the (mule) deer and the (pronghorn) antelope still play in these parts. And although the buffalo don't roam quite as freely as they used to, there are a few protected bison herds still residing in the Denver area, and they are quite the sight to see.

ACCESS AND REGULATIONS

The majority of trails detailed in the following pages are property of the City and County of Denver, although some might actually be located beyond city and county lines, and these are free of any access fees. A few hikes are located in state parks, managed by the Colorado Parks and Wildlife department, which require you to purchase a parking pass. Dogs are permitted in most cases, but must remain on a leash at all times for the safety of you, your dog, and the wildlife.

It is imperative to follow Leave No Trace guidelines at all times to help maintain the natural state of Denver's parks, trails, and waterways for continued enjoyment for all. These include staying on designated trails, proper disposal of waste (if there isn't a receptacle nearby, please carry trash with you until you find one), and respecting wildlife (please do not approach animals for any reason, pick wildflowers, or carve your initials into a tree). Take care of nature and it will take care of you. Please review the guidelines at colorado.com/CareForColorado to help ensure these trails, parks, and open spaces will remain enjoyable for years to come.

HOW TO USE THIS GUIDE

The hikes are presented in an easy-to-read format with at-a-glance information at the start. Each hike description contains the following information:

Hike number and name: The hike number is also shown on the location map to help you visualize the general location of the hike. We've used the official, or at least the commonly accepted, name for a trail or hike. Loop hikes or other routes that use several trails are usually named for the main trail or for a prominent feature along the way.

Overview: Each hike is introduced with a general description of the hike, including special attractions.

Elevation gain: This measurement indicates how much uphill climbing a trail requires. For example, a trail that is 1 mile long with an elevation gain of 1,000 feet is significantly steeper and more challenging than a trail that is 10 miles long with the same elevation gain.

Distance: This indicates the total distance of the hike in miles. Distances were carefully measured using the COTREX★★ (Colorado Trail Explorer) app, the state's unique trail-mapping database. Hikes may be loops, which use a series of trails so that you never retrace your steps; out and back, which return along the same trails used on the way out; and lollipops, which are hikes with an out-and-back section leading to a loop.

Hiking time: This approximate time in hours is necessarily based on an average hiking time for a reasonably fit person, or about 3 miles per hour. Non-hikers will take longer, and very fit, seasoned hikers will take less time. In some cases, hiking time is increased if there are a lot of points of interest or other activities to enjoy along the route.

Difficulty: All the hikes are rated as easy, moderate, or difficult, often with the reason for the rating. This is a subjective rating, but in general easy hikes can be done by nearly anyone and take a couple of hours at most. Because this guide features urban hikes, most of the trails are considered easy. Moderate hikes take a bit longer, usually due to a significant elevation gain or more challenging terrain. Difficult hikes are steep and take a considerable amount of time, creating the need to carry extra water, snacks, layers, and other necessities.

Seasons: All the trails in this urban hiking guide are accessible year-round, but always check local conditions before heading out. Annual seasonal closures are noted as necessary.

Trail surface: This section describes the surface underfoot: paved, dirt, gravel, sand, or boardwalk.

Land status: When hiking the trails described in this book, usually you'll be hiking on trails owned and managed by their respective cities and counties, which are available to use free of charge. The status of the land sometimes affects access or rules for use, specifically those in state parks or wildlife conservation areas.

Nearest town: This is the distance from the nearest town with at least a gas station and basic supplies.

Other trail users: Some of the hikes are on trails shared with joggers, horses, mountain bikes or e-bikes.

Water availability: It is recommended that hikers bring all the water they need from home, and that they bring more than they think necessary. Water sources are listed for each hike; however, in most cases these are only available from June through September, and are shut off in the winter (the same goes for restroom facilities, where available).

Canine compatibility: This section tells you if dogs are permitted or not, and whether they must be on a leash. Dogs are required to be leashed on all trails in the city of Denver.

Fees and permits: This section lists if a fee is required for trailhead parking.

Map: The official park or trail map is listed for each hike. These maps can be accessed online, and in many cases are available in hard copy form at the city or park visitor's center.

Trail contact: This section lists the name and contact information for the land-management agency that has jurisdiction over the hike. It's always a good idea to check with the agency before you hike to learn of trail closures, ongoing construction projects, or other unusual conditions.

Finding the trailhead: These driving directions are given in miles from downtown Denver, starting from Civic Center Park, followed by the GPS coordinates of the trailhead. In some cases, a trailhead name and address are also provided.

What to See: In this narrative, the hike is described in detail, along with interesting information about the area's history, geography, and notable points of interest. The description uses references to landmarks rather than distances wherever possible, since distances are listed under key points.

Miles and Directions: This is a listing of key points along the hike, including trail junctions and important landmarks. You should be able to follow the route by referencing this section; however, the key points are not a substitute for thoroughly reading the hike narrative before taking the trip. Distances are given from the start of the hike in miles.

★★Follow @UHDenver on COTREX to see the author's exact routes, as well as driving directions, elevation profiles, weather forecasts, and condition reports.

TRAIL FINDER

BEST PHOTOS

5. Mile High Loop at City Park
11. Ruby Hill Park Loop
16. Lake Mary and Lake Ladora at Rocky Mountain Arsenal National Wildlife Refuge
17. Wildlife Refuge Trail at Barr Lake State Park
22. High Line Canal Trail—East Orchard Road to Three Pond Park
31. Red Rocks Trail/Morrison Slide Loop
33. North Bison Overlook at Genesee Park
34. Lookout Mountain Park Loop
36. Peaks to Plains Trail—Clear Creek Canyon

WATER FEATURES

2. Cherry Creek Trail—Confluence Park to Sunken Gardens Park
3. South Platte River Trail—Cuernavaca Park to Johnson Habitat Park
4. Sloan's Lake Loop
5. Mile High Loop at City Park
6. Westerly Creek Trail
7. Bluff Lake Loop
8. Cherry Creek Trail—Cherry Creek Mall to Cherry Creek State Park
9. Washington Park Outer Loop
12. Sand Creek Greenway—Dahlia Trailhead to Havana Street
14. Ralston Creek Trail—Ralston Central Park to Gold Strike Park
16. Lake Mary and Lake Ladora at Rocky Mountain Arsenal National Wildlife Refuge
17. Wildlife Refuge Trail at Barr Lake State Park
18. Highline Canal Trail—Aurora City Center to Star K Ranch
19. Star K Ranch Double Loop
20. Toll Gate Creek Trail—Horseshoe Park to Quincy Reservoir
22. Highline Canal Trail—East Orchard Road to Three Pond Park
23. Mary Carter Greenway in South Platte Park
24. Chatfield Farms Loop
25. Piney Creek Trail—Piney Creek Trailhead to Larkspur Park
26. Clear Creek Trail—Wheat Ridge Greenbelt
27. Crown Hill Park Loop
29. Belmar Park Loop
30. Bear Creek Greenbelt
32. Evergreen Lake Loop
35. Clear Creek Trail—Downtown Golden (Peaks to Plains Trail)
36. Peaks to Plains Trail—Clear Creek Canyon

FINDING SOLITUDE

GOOD IN WINTER

Don't let the snow scare you—the Barr Lake rookery is most active January through April.

3. South Platte River Trail—Cuernavaca Park to Johnson Habitat Park
4. Sloan's Lake Loop
5. Mile High Loop at City Park
6. Westerly Creek Trail
7. Bluff Lake Loop
9. Washington Park Outer Loop
10. East Harvard Gulch Trail
11. Ruby Hill Park Loop
13. Van Bibber Creek Trail
14. Ralston Creek Trail—Ralston Central Park to Gold Strike Park
17. Wildlife Refuge Trail at Barr Lake State Park
18. High Line Canal Trail—Aurora City Center to Star K Ranch
20. Toll Gate Creek Trail—Horseshoe Park to Quincy Reservoir
22. High Line Canal Trail—East Orchard Road to Three Pond Park
23. Mary Carter Greenway in South Platte Park
25. Piney Creek Trail—Piney Creek Trailhead to Larkspur Park
27. Crown Hill Park Loop
29. Belmar Park Loop
32. Evergreen Lake Loop
33. North Bison Overlook at Genesee Park
35. Clear Creek Trail—Downtown Golden (Peaks to Plains Trail)
28. 40 West ArtLine

GREAT FOR KIDS
7. Bluff Lake Loop
9. Washington Park Outer Loop
19. Star K Ranch Double Loop
21. Soddie Loop at the Plains Conservation Center
23. Mary Carter Greenway in South Platte Park
24. Chatfield Farms Loop
29. Belmar Park Loop
32. Evergreen Lake Loop
33. North Bison Overlook at Genesee Park
28. 40 West ArtLine

BEST WILDLIFE VIEWING
7. Bluff Lake Loop
16. Lake Mary and Lake Ladora Loop at Rocky Mountain Arsenal National Wildlife Refuge
17. Wildlife Refuge Trail at Barr Lake State Park
19. Star K Ranch Double Loop
27. Crown Hill Park Loop
32. Evergreen Lake Loop
33. North Bison Overlook at Genesee Park
34. Lookout Mountain Park Loop

MAP LEGEND

Municipal

≡(25)≡	Interstate Highway
≡(287)≡	US Highway
≡(26)≡	State Road
———	County/Forest/Local Road
———	Paved Trail
- - - - -	Trail
⊢—+—⊣	Railroad
- - - - -	County Boundary

Featured Routes

═══	Featured Road
———	Featured Paved Trail
- - - - -	Featured Trail

Water Features

⬭	Lake/Body of Water
⸝⸜	Marsh/Swamp
∿	River/Creek

Symbols

⊔	Bridge
▲	Campground
○	City/Town
•—•	Gate
▬	Lodging
▲	Mountain/Peak
🅿	Parking
🛱	Picnic Area
■	Point of Interest
🚻	Restrooms
🔷	Scenic View
‖‖‖	Boardwalk
①	Trailhead
❓	Visitor Center

Land Management

▭	National Park/Forest
▣	State/City Park
⬚	Nature Center/Natural Area/Preserve

With the city skyline to the east and the mountains to the west, it's easy to see why the South Platte River Trail is so popular.

CENTRAL DENVER

Outdoor recreation is a top priority in Denver, and there are tons of hiking opportunities just steps from the busy city streets. In fact, the City and County of Denver manages more than 80 miles of trails and a whopping 19,000 acres of park space. It is also one of the few municipalities that employs a city forester and a city naturalist, responsible for the protection and regulation of public trees, open spaces, native plants, and wildlife habitats—all of which play a big role in water and air quality. The city is home to 126 state "Champion Trees" (the largest of their species in the state) and is committed to planting one million new trees by 2025 in an effort to broaden Denver's tree canopy, which is an important factor for the health of all urban areas, but especially in high-altitude locations where the sun and weather patterns are especially harsh.

Needless to say, the Mile High City has put a lot of effort into creating lovely, lush parks and trails for you to enjoy. Some of the trails in this section are located in a few particularly notable neighborhood parks, and some feature handpicked segments of the city's regional trail systems. Some aren't technically trails at all, but actually walking tours custom-designed to show off some of Denver's most impressive attractions, landmarks, and public artwork. Whether you live and work downtown, or are just visiting for a short time, there's a hike here to fit your needs.

A number of parks, creeks, and trees in and around downtown make it a breeze to find a pleasant place to stretch your legs.

1 DOWNTOWN LANDMARKS LOOP

This urban trail will lead you on a quick tour of some of Denver's most notable attractions. Starting at Union Station, with direct train service from the airport, this route is perfect for stretching your legs and seeing the sights during a long layover.

Elevation gain: 61 feet
Distance: 4.1-mile loop
Hiking time: About 2 hours
Difficulty: Easy
Seasons: Year-round
Trail surface: Paved
Land status: City and County of Denver
Nearest town: Denver (LoDo, Golden Triangle, 16th Street Mall neighborhoods)
Other trail users: Cars, joggers, cyclists
Water availability: No

Canine compatibility: Yes, on leash
Fees and permits: None
Map: Downtown Denver Attractions and Accommodations, assets.simpleviewinc.com/simpleview/image/upload/v1/clients/denver/VD_Downtown20_OVGs20_PRINT_f654bdf2-959d-49df-901e-63ec255c94fd.pdf
Trail contact: City of Denver: (720) 913-1311
Trailhead GPS: N39 45.17' / E104 59.97'

FINDING THE TRAILHEAD

From Civic Center Park in downtown Denver, take Speer Boulevard north for about 1 mile, then turn right on Wynkoop Street. Union Station will be on your left. Park on the street or at any of the surrounding parking garages downtown. To arrive by train (light rail) from Denver International Airport, take the A Line west toward Union Station. (Union Station: 1701 Wynkoop St., Denver)

WHAT TO SEE

Whether you're new to town or just passing through, this hike will lead you on a quick walking tour to see some of Denver's top attractions and landmarks—both old and new—in just a few hours. You'll travel from the heart of LoDo (a nickname for Lower Downtown), one of the most well-known, historic, and hip neighborhoods in town, to the Golden Triangle, the city's hub of political and cultural activity. Although the route can technically be completed in about 1.5 hours from a purely distance perspective, be sure to allow extra time for shopping, dining, loitering, and taking pictures along the way. For those with time to spare, this could easily turn into a full-day excursion!

Union Station serves as your "trailhead" and is also the first landmark stop on the tour. Built in 1881 as a hub for the burgeoning railroad system, this was once the largest and most grandiose structure in the West. After the building was added to the National Register of Historic Places in 1974 and renovated in 2014, it reclaimed its splendor as a transit center for the city's light rail and regional Amtrak systems. The mesmerizing structure is also home to the elegant Crawford Hotel as well as some of the city's most highly acclaimed restaurants and bars, making it a great hangout space.

From Union Station, begin walking southwest on Wynkoop Street. Turn right at the corner and walk northwest on 16th Street, then climb the stairs up to the cable-stayed Millennium Bridge for a glimpse of Commons Park and the distant mountains. After

With a direct light rail route to the Denver International Airport, the magnificent Union Station is a great jumping-off point from which to explore the city by foot.

marveling at the footbridge's unique design and the impressive views, return to Wynkoop Street and turn right once again. Turn left at the next corner and stroll southeast down 15th Street, noticing the preserved redbrick architecture and antique-looking murals, reminiscent of the area's early days. In four blocks, turn right on Larimer Street and walk through Larimer Square. Named for General Larimer, who founded Denver City in 1858, what was the region's original Main Street is now a popular shopping and dining destination charmingly adorned with string lights and flags year-round.

At the end of the block, turn left on 14th Street. Immediately on your right is the University of Colorado–Denver campus building, followed in a few blocks by the Denver Center for the Performing Arts, an architecturally interesting complex housing several theaters, an opera house, and a few restaurants that offers internationally acclaimed shows year-round. Turn right to walk through the cavernous courtyard and see the outdoor sculpture park on the southwest end of the structure.

Continuing down 14th Street, next you'll come upon a most unusual sight: a giant blue bear peering into the windows of the Colorado Convention Center, Denver's state-of-the-art meeting, event, and concert venue. This strikingly lovable 40-foot sculpture titled *I See What You Mean* is one of 300-plus public art pieces that have been amassed since the enactment of a public art funding initiative in 1988 (see the full collection at denverpublicart.org).

Continue walking southeast down 14th Street until it dead-ends at Colfax Avenue, the longest commercial street in America, and one of Denver's most infamous thoroughfares. Cross the road and take a slight right turn onto Bannock Street, walking south. You are

Left: Civic Center Park is the traditional epicenter of the city, flanked by the Colorado State Capitol and the Denver City Council buildings, and surrounded by art and history museums. Right: Despite the many major international events that take place at the Colorado Convention Center year after year, the Big Blue Bear always steals the show.

now at the epicenter of Denver's Golden Triangle district, around which the majority of local and state government activity takes place. On your left is Civic Center Park, a historic green space stretching between the Denver City Council building to the west and the Colorado State Capitol to the east, featuring 25,000 square feet of flower beds, mature trees, and an impressive classic Greek amphitheater. The park is often buzzing with events such as a holiday Christkindl Market, food truck roundups, and live music performances.

At the south end of the park, cross West 14th Avenue and continue straight on Bannock Street. Turn left on West 13th Avenue for a quick jaunt past some of Denver's finest cultural attractions: the Denver Art Museum, Denver Public Library, and History Colorado Center, to name a few. At the next corner, turn left on Broadway, another major Denver thoroughfare. Once back in Civic Center Park, you gain a better view of the gold-plated dome of the capitol building, a nod to the state's rich mining history.

Continue down Broadway until you come to 16th Street, located across from the Civic Center transit station, then turn left. Designed by renowned architect I. M. Pei, the 16th Street pedestrian mall is an attraction in itself, with a slew of shopping, dining, and entertainment options, including an eclectic variety of street performers, public artwork, a movie theater, and a bowling alley. A free "Mall Ride" trolley shuttles people up and down the 14-block stretch, with the opportunity to hop on and off every few blocks, so feel free to hitch a lift if you're in a hurry.

At Blake Street, turn right and walk 4 blocks northeast until you reach 20th Street. Before you now is Coors Field, home to the Colorado Rockies baseball team and one of the most consistently well-attended stadiums in the league. Spectators are treated with mountain views from the first base line section as well as from the venue's lively rooftop bar, and rumor has it that the high-altitude location creates ideal conditions for an above average amount of home run hits. Turn left at 20th, then left again on the next corner at Wazee Street. A final right turn on 17th Street will deliver you back to Union Station, completing the loop tour.

MILES AND DIRECTIONS

0.0 Starting in front of Union Station, begin walking southwest on Wynkoop Street.

0.09 Turn right on 16th Street.

0.29 Walk up to the top of the Millennium Bridge, then retrace your steps back down to the corner of Wynkoop and 16th Streets.

0.49 Turn right on Wynkoop Street.

0.59 Turn left on 15th Street.

0.85 Turn right on Larimer Street (Larimer Square).

Denver's LoDo district is characterized by its collection of preserved redbrick, industrial-style buildings, many of which still feature the historic murals and signs from the original inhabitants of the late 1800s and early 1900s.

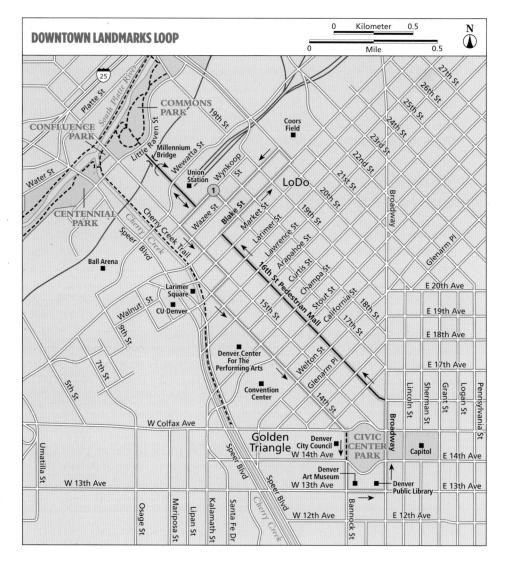

DOWNTOWN LANDMARKS LOOP

0.95 Turn left on 14th Street.

1.1 Arrive at the Denver Center for the Performing Arts. Continue straight.

1.3 Arrive at the Colorado Convention Center.

1.6 Cross Colfax Avenue and take a slight right turn onto Bannock Street.

1.8 Cross West 14th Avenue Parkway to continue south on Bannock Street.

1.9 Turn left on West 13th Avenue.

2.1 Turn left on Broadway.

2.2 Cross West 14th Avenue Parkway, continuing north on Broadway.

2.3 Cross Colfax Avenue and continue north on Broadway.

2.4 Turn left down 16th Street.

3.3 Turn right on Blake Street.

3.7 When you reach Coors Field at 20th Street, turn left.

3.8 Turn left on Wazee Street.

4.0 Turn right on 17th Street.

4.1 Arrive back at Union Station.

LOCAL INTEREST

The Cruise Room: Located inside the Oxford Hotel, this elegant watering hole opened in 1933. Its art deco interior and Prohibition-era cocktail list offer a refreshing respite from LoDo's bevy of sports bars and breweries. 1600 17th St., Denver; (303) 262-6070; theoxfordhotel.com/eat-drink/the-cruise-room

Sam's No. 3: A Denver classic since 1927, this hopping 24-hour diner continues to be a local favorite thanks to an all-encompassing menu that satisfies large appetites for breakfast, lunch, dinner, and literally everything in between. 435 S. Cherry St., Glendale; (303) 333-4403; samsno3.com

Rockmount Ranch Wear: This Western retailer has been outfitting celebrities with high-quality bandanas, cowboy hats, bolo ties, shirts, and other authentic necessities since 1946, and claims to have invented and popularized the snap-button shirt. 1626 Wazee St., Denver; (800) 776-2566; rockmount.com

The Dairy Block: A revived historic warehouse turned hip "micro-district," the Dairy Block features a pedestrian alleyway lined with independent shops, restaurants, and art galleries—all of which you can peruse with drink in hand from any of the six resident cocktail bars within the block's boundaries. 1800 Wazee St., Denver; (303) 309-4817; dairyblock.com

LODGING

Crawford Hotel: Located inside Union Station, this boutique hotel is unique and chic—and you don't even have to leave the building to access some of the hottest bars and restaurants in the city. If you do wish to step off-site, the complimentary Tesla house car will whisk you wherever you need to go in town. 1701 Wynkoop St., Denver; (720) 460-3700; thecrawfordhotel.com

The ART Hotel: Contemporary Golden Triangle accommodations just steps from some of the city's top cultural attractions and featuring a hip rooftop bar. 1201 Broadway Ave., Denver; (303) 572-8000; hilton.com/en/hotels/denrtqq-the-art-hotel-denver

2 CHERRY CREEK TRAIL— CONFLUENCE PARK TO SUNKEN GARDENS PARK

The Cherry Creek Trail is one of Denver's most iconic urban paths— a must-see for visitors and a go-to trail for locals. This first section of the 45-mile regional trail passes through the downtown corridor, hugging the bank of its meandering namesake water feature and offering an interesting tour of notable landmarks, public art, and urban wildlife along the way.

Elevation gain: 59 feet
Distance: 4.0 miles out and back
Hiking time: About 1.5 hours
Difficulty: Easy
Seasons: Year-round
Trail surface: Paved
Land status: City and County of Denver
Nearest town: Denver (LoDo, Speer neighborhoods)
Other trail users: Cyclists, joggers
Water availability: No

Canine compatibility: Yes, on leash
Fees and permits: None
Map: Denver Regional Trail Map: denvergov.org/content/dam/ denvergov/Portals/747/documents/ parks/trails/DPR-regional-trail-map .pdf
Trail contact: Denver Parks & Recreation: (720) 913-1311
Trailhead GPS: N39 45.24' / E105 00.47'

FINDING THE TRAILHEAD

From downtown Denver, drive north on Speer Boulevard for about 1 mile. Turn right on Wewatta Street, then left on 15th Street. Street parking is available along Little Raven Street.

WHAT TO SEE

The Cherry Creek Trail is best known for its ease of access and pleasant scenery, and is often crowded with joggers, cyclists, and dog walkers. Whether you're a first-time visitor or a longtime local, the path—which connects downtown Denver to Castlewood Canyon State Park, located about 37 miles southeast of the city—offers users a brush with nature just steps away from the busy city streets and neighborhoods. Bicycle commuters are especially fond of this regional route, and a thoughtful design separates cyclists and pedestrians for safety and efficiency, with the creek dividing the trail into two paths throughout this 2-mile section. As such, follow signage and stick to the east side as much as possible if you're on foot to avoid colliding with any whizzing wheels.

This section covers a 2-mile stretch between the trail's origin at Confluence Park and Sunken Gardens Park—both historic landmarks and attractions in their own right. Although there are no restrooms or water fountains available on the trail, there are several ramps providing city access, putting ample services and amenities at your fingertips. You'll start at Confluence Park—at once a green space as well as a "natural" water park development where people gather to fish, float, and run the man-made kayak course on the South Platte River. Across the water to the north sits the cavernous REI store,

This timeless urban trail keeps evolving as the city of Denver continues to experience phenomenal growth.

housed in a historic brick railyard building (accessible via a footbridge on the western corner of the park, if you care to do some shopping or get a closer look at the building's neat architecture).

Begin your hike by walking down a ramp south of the footbridge, making sure to stay to the left on the pedestrian-only side of the trail north of the creek. This entire section of the trail runs parallel to Speer Boulevard, one of the city's main thoroughfares, but you'll hardly notice the traffic noise as the trail sits about 20 feet below the street and just feet away from the babbling Cherry Creek. Retaining walls on both sides of the gully present ideal canvases for street artists, and you'll see many iterations of Denver life in an array of colors and mediums throughout the hike. Juxtaposing these bold, modern murals is the serenity of the flora and fauna that flourishes in and around the creek banks. In springtime, pink and white cherry blossoms drape over the trail, and the creek is dotted with ducks, geese, and otters.

Don't forget to look up and to the south from time to time to check out landmarks such as the Ball Arena, a major concert venue and home to the Denver Nuggets basketball team; the Auraria Higher Education Center, home to three separate colleges and universities, as well as the Tivoli Brewing Company, one of the city's first craft brewers; and eventually the historic cloister of Denver West High School rising over Sunken Gardens Park, which serves as your turnaround point.

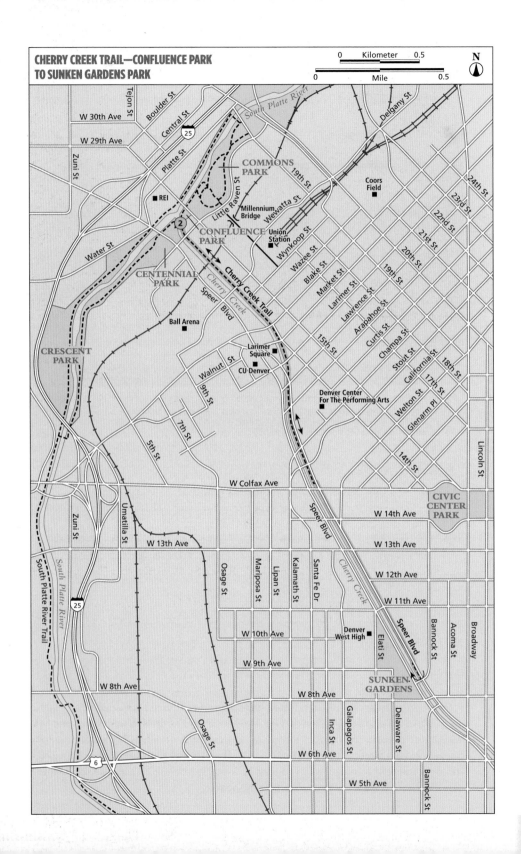

0   Kilometer   0.5

0   Mile   0.5

N

A popular bike commuter route, this section of the trail is divided to safely separate pedestrians and cyclists.

MILES AND DIRECTIONS

0.0 Locate the paved path south of Confluence Park. Begin by descending a ramp south of the bridge. Stay to the left on the pedestrian-only side of the creek.

2.0 Turn around at the Bannock Street bridge and retrace your steps back to your starting point, or continue straight on the trail as long as you'd like.

4.0 Arrive back at Confluence Park.

LOCAL INTEREST

My Brother's Bar: Although the building has changed hands several times, this is well known as the oldest bar in Denver and has been continuously serving beers and burgers since 1873. 2376 15th St., Denver; (303) 455-9991; mybrothersbar.com

Menya Ramen and Poke: This modern, quick-service kitchen is locally owned and operated and specializes in a variety of Asian-fusion favorites like kimchi, pork buns, and build-your-own poke bowls. 1590 Little Raven St. #170, Denver; (720) 696-6769; menyacolorado.com/copy-of-menya-sushi

Denver Museum of Contemporary Art: This small but entertaining attraction features five galleries on two floors, plus a rooftop cafe and bar. 1485 Delgany St., Denver; (303) 298-7554; mcadenver.org

LODGING

Kimpton Hotel Born: Walk to the trailhead from this upscale boutique hotel located in one of the trendiest parts of town, surrounded by amazing restaurants, shops, and entertainment options. 1600 Wewatta St., Denver; (303) 323-0024; hotelborndenver.com

The Mint House: Treat yourself to a stay at this swanky, modern high-rise for a taste of the hip, city-dweller lifestyle. You'll get a full apartment to yourself, plus access to a state-of-the-art fitness center and rooftop swimming pool. 1777 Chestnut Pl., Denver; (855) 972-9090; minthouse.com/downtown-denver

3 SOUTH PLATTE RIVER TRAIL—CUERNAVACA PARK TO JOHNSON HABITAT PARK

Take a stroll down one of Denver's most iconic and populated urban trails, full of people, parks, history, wildlife, and landmarks in the heart of the city.

Elevation gain: 71 feet
Distance: 9.3 miles out and back
Hiking time: About 3 hours
Difficulty: Easy
Seasons: Year-round
Trail surface: Paved
Land status: City of Denver
Nearest town: Denver (LoDo, Sun Valley, Baker neighborhoods)
Other trail users: Cyclists
Water availability: Yes, at trailhead

Canine compatibility: Yes, on leash
Fees and permits: None
Map: Denver Bike Map: denvergov .org/content/dam/denvergov/ Portals/708/documents/2019 -Denver-Bike-Map.pdf
Trail contact: Denver Parks and Recreation: (720) 913-1311
Trailhead GPS: N39 45.82' / E105 00.05'

FINDING THE TRAILHEAD

From downtown Denver, drive west on 20th Street for about 1 mile. Turn left on Little Raven Street, then right on 19th Street. Turn right at the stop sign on Rockmont Street and park either along the street or in the parking lot adjacent to the apartment building, beyond the roundabout. (City of Cuernavaca Park: 3500 Rockmont Dr., Denver)

WHAT TO SEE

Undoubtedly one of the most popular recreational paths in the Denver metro area, the South Platte River Trail stretches 32 miles north to south between the cities of Brighton and Littleton. Not to be confused with the Colorado Scenic and Historic Byway by the same name, a driving route located in the northeast corner of the state, this section of trail goes right through downtown Denver and showcases several parks and attractions along the way. It is a great example of how valuable urban trails are to providing city dwellers a chance to connect to the natural world, even if just for a few steps or moments.

You'll start at the city of Cuernavaca Park, named for one of Denver's several sister cities, hiking south on the paved path. This is a popular route for bike commuters, so be sure to stick to the right of the trail to allow enough room for cyclists to zoom past. At times there are natural-surface side paths you can use to step away from the pavement every now and then if you prefer. At first you will pass through a very vibrant part of Denver, home to many apartment homes, office buildings, bars, restaurants, and shops. On the other side of 20th Street you'll have a view of Commons Park from across the river. Commons Park flows right into Confluence Park, aptly named for the spot where the South Platte River and Cherry Creek merge waters. This park is also known for its unique paddling course, swimming beach, and public artwork. On your right is the massive REI store, housed in a historic brick railyard facility, which is worth a look around

Confluence Park is a lively urban waterfront park in downtown Denver where the South Platte River and Cherry Creek merge.

the inside if you have time. All of these parks are usually very crowded with people jogging, walking dogs, playing volleyball, having picnics, people watching, and generally enjoying some space away from the surrounding high-rise buildings.

The bridge on the south end of this trio of parks begins the Cherry Creek Trail, another popular regional thoroughfare that connects downtown Denver to Franktown, some 45 miles south of the city. After passing underneath Speer Boulevard, you'll enter a "Miracle Mile" of sorts, where some of the city's top attractions and activities are located in quick succession. Across the water you'll see the collection of roller coasters, rides, and waterslides that make up the Elitch Gardens amusement park, which first opened as a private zoo in 1890. Straight ahead you can get a glimpse inside Empower Field at Mile High, home to the Denver Broncos football team, in the distance. Soon after, you'll pass the Denver Aquarium and Children's Museum on the right.

Soon the crowds will clear and you will find yourself strolling quietly alongside the wide, slow flow of the South Platte River. Once a lush watering hole for wildlife and campsite for Native American tribes and hunters, the riverside became populated with a bustling mining town during the gold rush in the 1850s. In 1965 the river rose to catastrophic levels during a summer rainstorm that resulted in $540 million in damages and a downfall for the riverbed, which was left full of trash and debris once the swell settled. The Greenway Foundation was established in the 1970s to revitalize the stream corridor, resulting in the creation of the more than 100 acres of park space and 100 miles of multiuse trails that exist today.

This public art piece, titled *Sun Spot*, is positioned facing the trail in front of the Denver Animal Shelter and is made entirely of stainless steel dog tags.

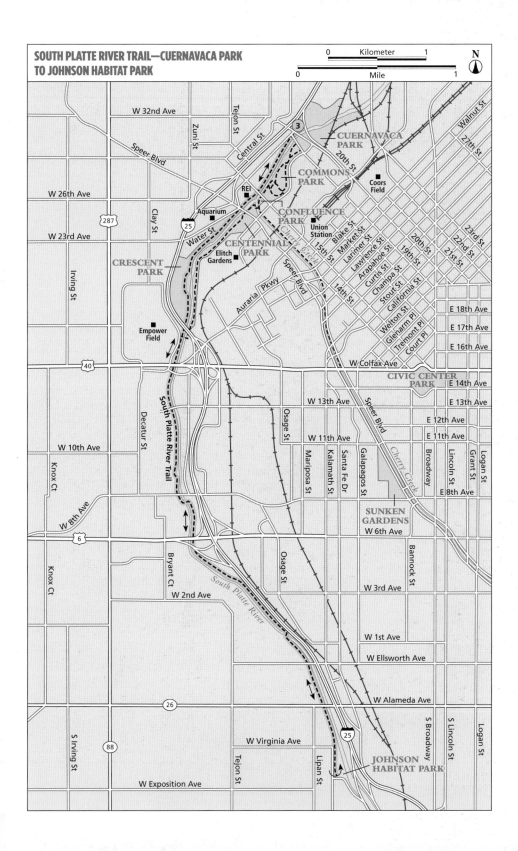

As you reach the I-25 freeway underpass you'll find yourself directly in front of the football stadium, offering a different perspective of the iconic statue of a white mustang perched above the entrance. Eventually the trail will parallel the freeway closely, which makes things a bit noisy but still offers lovely views of the river. Soon you'll arrive at the Johnson Habitat Park, an innovative environmental education area with river access for fishing and floating. This is your turnaround point, although the trail stretches on for several miles more until it reaches the city of Littleton, where it turns into the Mary Carter Greenway Trail and continues even farther toward the South Platte Reservoir.

MILES AND DIRECTIONS

0.0 Access the paved path on the southeast corner of Cuernavaca Park. Begin hiking southwest, under 20th Street.

2.6 Cross the bridge to the left, then turn right.

3.7 Cross the bridge to the right, then turn left.

4.7 Arrive at Johnson Habitat Park. Turn around and retrace your steps to the trailhead.

9.3 Arrive back at the trailhead.

LOCAL INTEREST

Raices Brewing: With a large, shady patio, direct trail access, and a rotating selection of local food trucks, this neighborhood spot is a great choice for post-hike refreshments with Latin flair. 2060 W. Colfax Ave., Denver; (720) 324-8550; raicesbrewing.com

Avanti Food and Beverage: Denver's first food hall is still one of its best thanks to a stellar rooftop patio, spacious bar area, and wide range of local eateries to choose from, cafeteria-style. 3200 Pecos St., Denver; (720) 269-4778; avantifandb.com

Stranahan's Colorado Whiskey: Stop by this distillery for a tour and taste of its award-winning single malt in a charming, rustic-industrial lounge. 200 S. Kalamath St., Denver; (303) 296-7440; stranahans.com

LODGING

The Comma Hotel: Overlooking Cuernavaca Park, this innovative lodging property gets its name from the unique shape of the building and offers guests a home-away-from-home experience with luxury bedding, full kitchens, and locally sourced decor. 330 Mariposa St., Denver; (303) 284-5551; ecghotels.com/about

4 SLOAN'S LAKE LOOP

Bustling Sloan's Lake Park offers sweeping views of both the city and mountains, as well as an interesting glimpse of life in some of Denver's hottest neighborhoods.

Elevation gain: 8 feet
Distance: 2.8-mile loop
Hiking time: About 1 hour
Difficulty: Easy
Seasons: Year-round
Trail surface: Paved
Land status: City and County of Denver
Nearest town: Denver (Sloan's Lake neighborhood)
Other trail users: Cyclists, joggers
Water availability: Yes

Canine compatibility: Dogs must remain on leash
Fees and permits: None
Map: Denver Parks & Recreation
Map: denvergov.org/content/dam/denvergov/Portals/747/documents/parks/trails/Sloans_Lake_Loop.pdf
Trail contact: Denver Parks & Recreation: (720) 913-1311
Trailhead GPS: N39 44.73' / E105 02.70'

FINDING THE TRAILHEAD

From downtown Denver, drive west on Colfax Avenue for about 1.5 miles. Take a slight right onto Federal Boulevard, then left on West 17th Avenue. Turn right into the parking area at Utica Street in about 1.5 miles. The trail begins north of the parking area, near the lake.

WHAT TO SEE

Sloan's Lake is one of Denver's largest public parks, and, thanks to its elevated location on the western border of the city, it offers spectacular views of the downtown skyline as well as the foothills. The park is usually busy with people walking dogs, jogging, Rollerblading, having picnics, and playing sports, which means it's also great for people watching. The lake was formed in 1861 when a farmer accidentally struck a natural spring while digging a well—giving it the original nickname of "Sloan's Leak"—and in the years following became a popular place for swimming, boating, fishing, and ice skating. These activities can still be enjoyed today, but increased residential and commercial development in the area has led to rising bacteria levels in the lake water, and the lake itself is sometimes closed to recreation. Still, it offers a nice place to stroll. You'll begin your hike on the south side of the lake, moving clockwise. The main trail is paved and divided with a painted white line for safety, but occasionally you will also have the option to veer slightly off course on a crushed gravel path (and you might especially prefer this route if the main path is busy with cyclists).

Starting out you'll pass a few soccer fields before coming to an arched bridge. Be sure to stop here and look to the east for a nice view of the city skyline. Turning north, the trail runs parallel to Sheridan Boulevard. On your left sits the small town of Edgewater, a burgeoning residential area with a variety of building styles, from Victorian homes to modern duplexes, and a nice collection of funky shops and restaurants tucked between rows of homes. When you come to the corner of Sheridan Boulevard and Byron Place, you can see a marquee marking the entrance to the city's main drag on your left. Now

Even the birds have a better view from Sloan's Lake Park.

you are heading east, through a meadow, as you approach a boathouse, which was once the centerpiece of a variety of attractions including an amusement park, garden, dance hall, and menagerie. Today the boathouse hosts the largest Dragon Boat Festival in the country, an annual two-day event that attracts more than 100,000 people to enjoy food vendors, dance performances, and, of course, decorative boat races, all designed to celebrate Asian American heritage. Just beyond the boat dock you'll see a shaded viewing platform jutting out over the lake. This is a nice place to take a break and spend a moment looking for various bird species on the lake, and you'll likely see various species of geese and ducks, among others.

After rounding the northeast corner and heading south, you are in for a treat: panoramic views of the Front Range foothills. Here the park tends to be a bit less crowded and more secluded, as it is farther away from the main roads, parking area, and boat dock. Slow down and take your time while marveling at the mountain scenery. You'll also notice a small island in the lake that attracts a variety of wildlife, so keep your eyes peeled. Although it is really just one body of water, this southeast section is technically known as Cooper Lake. After rounding the southeast corner and crossing another footbridge, you'll soon arrive back at the parking area to complete your trek.

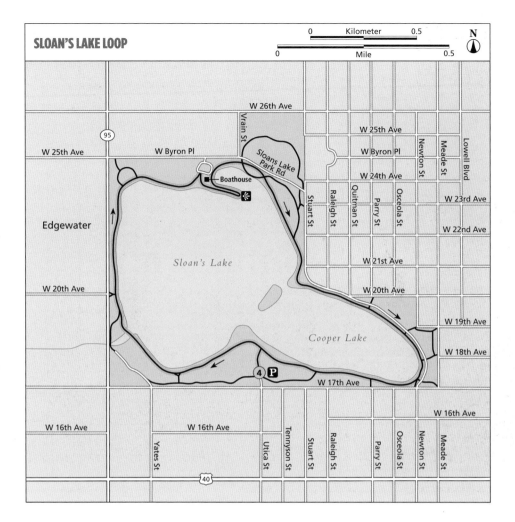

MILES AND DIRECTIONS

0.0 Locate the trail north of the parking lot and start hiking west, with the lake on your right.

0.45 Cross the bridge near the corner of 17th Avenue and Sheridan Boulevard and continue north.

0.87 At the northwest corner of the park, near the intersection of Sheridan Boulevard and West Byron Place, stay right to continue on the trail past the parking area.

1.1 When you arrive at the boathouse and docks, stay right to venture down to the observation platform. Retrace your steps back from the platform and turn right back at the boathouse to resume the loop. Continue to hug the lake on your right to return to the parking area.

2.8 Arrive back at the trailhead.

A peninsular promenade takes you off the beaten path.

LOCAL INTEREST

Joyride Brewery: This neighborhood hot spot has around sixteen craft beers on tap and a rooftop patio overlooking the park. A rotating schedule of local food trucks is available on-site daily for food pairings. 2501 Sheridan Blvd., Edgewater; (720) 432-7560; joyridebrewing.com

Edgewater Public Market: This uber-hip dining hall meets shopping mall combo is the area's latest and greatest one-stop-shop concept, where you'll find vendors selling everything from Ethiopian food to knitting supplies and everything in between. 5505 W. 20th Ave., Edgewater; edgewaterpublicmarket.com

LODGING

Beautifully Curated Home on the Park (Airbnb): This Airbnb Plus property offers an entire home and patio to yourself, smartly styled with mid-century modern decor and just steps away from the Sloan's Lake Loop trailhead. airbnb.com/rooms/plus/12210358?source_impression_id=p3_1610479657_On%2FNs%2B5ZTTy7jG26

5 MILE HIGH LOOP AT CITY PARK

This route provides a historic tour around City Park, Denver's oldest and most expansive green space with some of the best and most iconic views of the city skyline.

Elevation gain: Minimal
Distance: 3.2-mile loop
Hiking time: 1–2 hours
Difficulty: Easy
Seasons: Year-round
Trail surface: Paved, dirt, gravel
Land status: City and County of Denver
Nearest town: Denver (City Park neighborhood)
Other trail users: Joggers, cyclists
Water availability: Yes

Canine compatibility: Dogs must remain on leash
Fees and permits: None
Map: City Park Trail Map: denvergov.org/files/assets/public/parks-and-recreation/documents/trails/city_park_loops.pdf
Trail contact: Denver Parks and Recreation: (720) 913-1311
Trailhead GPS: N39 44.85' / E104 56.92'

FINDING THE TRAILHEAD

 From downtown Denver, drive east on 17th Avenue for about 1.5 miles, then turn left on Josephine Street. Take a right onto East 23rd Avenue in about 0.5 mile, then turn right at the fork. The parking lot is on your left just past Ferril Lake.

WHAT TO SEE

Designed in 1882 with a similar layout to New York City's Central Park, Denver's City Park is home to some of the city's top attractions, including the Denver Zoo and the Denver Museum of Nature & Science. At 330 acres, it is the largest park in Denver and also features a public golf course, two lakes, sports fields, and several historic monuments—making for a varied and interesting place for a stroll. Although many of the park's features were constructed in the late 1800s, this particular trail wasn't created until 2009 to showcase the area's numerous monuments, many of which can be easily overlooked.

Right away you'll notice the smaller of the two lakes, Duck Lake, adjacent to where the trail begins. Whether you prefer to take a gander at the beginning or end of your hike is up to you, but be sure to spend some time gazing at this rookery behind the zoo, where you are likely to spot an array of birdlife. Heading southwest on the trail, the first and probably most notable points of interest will come into view on your left just after clearing the parking area: the City Park Pavilion. This lakefront pavilion and boathouse have served as a popular central gathering place for more than a century. These days it plays host to a live jazz concert series that draws crowds on Sunday evenings in the summertime. Continuing on, you'll pass two small gardens before arriving at a roundabout with an impressive statue of Martin Luther King Jr. at its center. Beyond this landmark the trail meanders through a spacious meadow—often occupied by sunbathers, picnic blankets, and volleyball nets—and past a children's playground as it turns north toward the golf course (actually located across the street from the park).

This bench is perfectly placed to watch the sunset over the Rocky Mountains.

After passing the tennis courts and rounding the northwest corner of the park boundary, turning left to move south along York Street, you'll soon come to a fork in the trail. Veer left and stroll through a corridor of old-growth cottonwood trees. As you cross 21st Avenue, notice the Gothic-style walls of the McClellan Gateway, and the Graham-Bible House, which was originally constructed in 1892 for the park superintendent's family and exemplifies an architectural trend of that time known as Victorian Queen Anne "Shingle" style. The home was later designated as a Denver Historic Landmark and currently serves as the home base for the parks department's Outdoor Recreation Program.

The shady trail meanders south a little farther before turning east, leading you across the City Park Esplanade. On your left sits the Thatcher Fountain, whose basin sits at exactly 5,280 feet above sea level, in honor of Denver's "Mile High" moniker. On your right sprawls the historic campus of Denver's East High School, one of the city's first high schools. Constructed in 1925 in a colonial-style architecture that was popular on the East Coast at the time, the building is still in use and was also added to the collection of Denver Historic Landmarks in 1991.

Next, the trail winds through another field before turning east by the south side of Ferril Lake. Here there are several different paths you can take that all go the same direction: a paved inner path for cyclists or a gravel one that parallels 17th Avenue. You'll turn left when you reach Colorado Boulevard, and again just before reaching the entrance to the science museum, to explore an area that once served as the original botanic gardens. Here you'll notice towering evergreen trees and a variety of other species offering ample shade and serenity despite the heavily trafficked road nearby. Continue northwest on the path of your choice (again, there are several here that weave across each other, all ultimately leading back to the lake and trailhead), making sure to stop and gaze to the west for one of the most photographed scenes of the Denver skyline, with the snowcapped Rocky Mountains as a backdrop.

Eventually the trail will come to hug the banks of the lake, once a popular place for toy boat races and canoeing. You'll see the boathouse across the water, behind which sits the pavilion and the trailhead parking area.

MILES AND DIRECTIONS

- **0.0** Locate the trail on the northwest corner of the parking area. Begin walking south/southwest on the dirt path.
- **0.15** Cross the pavement leading to the Martin Luther King Jr. statue on your left, and continue on the dirt path through the meadow.

Ferril Lake provides a scenic spot for fishing and picnics.

Don't forget to take a gander at the array of waterfowl that gather on Duck Lake.

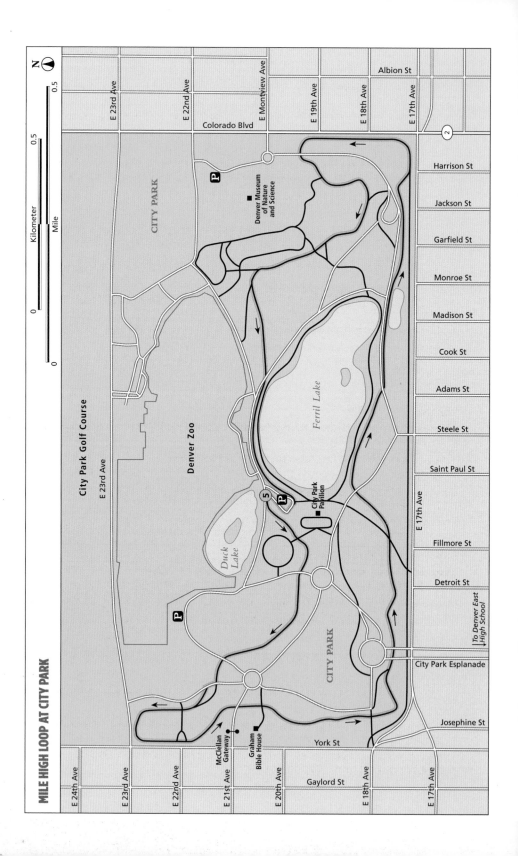

MILE HIGH LOOP AT CITY PARK

E 24th Ave
E 23rd Ave
E 22nd Ave
E 21st Ave
E 20th Ave
E 18th Ave
E 17th Ave

Gaylord St
York St
Josephine St
City Park Esplanade
Detroit St
Fillmore St
E 17th Ave
Saint Paul St
Steele St
Adams St
Cook St
Madison St
Monroe St
Garfield St
Jackson St
Harrison St

Albion St
E 17th Ave
E 18th Ave
E 19th Ave
E Montview Ave
E 22nd Ave
E 23rd Ave

Colorado Blvd

CITY PARK

City Park Golf Course

E 23rd Ave

Denver Zoo

Duck Lake

Ferril Lake

Denver Museum of Nature and Science

City Park Pavilion

CITY PARK

McClellan Gateway

Graham Bible House

To Denver East High School

N

Kilometer
0   0.5
Mile
0   0.5

2

5

0.38 Continue north on the path, crossing several paved routes leading toward the tennis courts on your right.

0.6 Follow the dirt path around the corner to the left, and continue south on the route parallel to York Street.

0.75 Veer left to follow the path toward the interior of the park, through a grove of cottonwood trees.

0.85 Cross 21st Avenue to continue on the trail, past the McClellan Gates and Graham-Bible House structures.

1.1 Follow the path around the corner to the left and past the Thatcher Memorial Fountain.

1.5 Cross the road and continue east on the trail, with Ferril Lake on your left.

1.7 Cross the road again to stay on the path, continuing east.

2.2 Turn left when you reach Colorado Boulevard, continuing north.

2.3 Veer left onto a dirt path and across a small street before continuing to the southwest.

2.6 Follow the trail as it turns north again, with the lake to the southwest and the museum to the northeast.

2.8 Stay left to continue around the meadow, heading east toward the lake.

3.0 Follow the path around the north side of Ferril Lake, heading west.

3.2 Arrive back at the trailhead/parking area.

LOCAL INTEREST

Atomic Cowboy and the Denver Biscuit Company: This local favorite specializes in towering breakfast sandwiches by day and heavenly pizza slices by night, with a full bar to boot. 3237 E. Colfax Ave., Denver; (303) 377-7900; atomiccowboy.net

Vine Street Pub & Brewery: Enjoy friendly service, juicy burgers, and jam music at this classic Colorado hangout. 1700 Vine St., Denver; (303) 388-2337; mountainsunpub.com

City Park Farmers Market: Swing by this open-air affair to purchase a local food souvenir or pick up picnic fixins to take into the park. Open Saturday mornings from May through October. cityparkfarmersmarket.com

Tattered Cover Bookstore: The Colfax location of Denver's beloved independent bookseller is housed in a renovated theater, with an on-site cafe and cozy atmosphere that lures visitors in to mingle among its historic stacks for hours on end. 2526 E. Colfax Ave., Denver; (303) 322-7727; tatteredcover.com

LODGING

Adagio Bed & Breakfast: A charming Victorian property with well-appointed rooms, a quaint outdoor patio, and fabulous food on-site. 1430 Race St., Denver; (720) 531-2169; adagiodenverbb.com

Private Carriage House (Airbnb): This historic carriage house building has been beautifully updated with modern fixtures while retaining its vintage charm with features such as exposed brick walls. airbnb.com/rooms/21097394?s=67&unique_share_id =ad30b772-24b4-4f28-ba3e-f889d425115e

6 WESTERLY CREEK TRAIL

This urban greenway meanders through a riparian corridor offering recreationists a chance to immerse themselves in nature in the middle of one of the hottest neighborhoods in the Denver area.

Elevation gain: 53 feet
Distance: 2.0-mile loop
Hiking time: About 1 hour
Difficulty: Easy
Seasons: Year-round
Trail surface: Paved
Land status: City and County of Denver
Nearest town: Denver (Central Park neighborhood)
Other trail users: Cyclists, joggers
Water availability: Yes, at trailhead

Canine compatibility: Yes, on leash
Fees and permits: None
Map: Denver Parks & Recreation Westerly Creek Park Map: denvergov .org/content/dam/denvergov/ Portals/747/documents/ParkArt/ ParkArt_Westerly%20Creek%20Park .pdf
Trail contact: Denver Parks & Recreation: (720) 913-1311
Trailhead GPS: N39 45.64' / E104 52.74'

FINDING THE TRAILHEAD

From downtown Denver, take I-70 East for about 4 miles to exit 278 onto Quebec Street/CO 35. Turn right on Quebec Street. In about 1 mile turn left on Martin Luther King Jr. Boulevard. In 1 more mile, turn left on Beeler Street, then left into the Central Park parking lot.

WHAT TO SEE

Central Park (formerly known as Stapleton, named for the Stapleton International Airport that served as the area's primary airport until 1995) is Denver's largest neighborhood, consisting of twelve master-planned residential communities and over 1,100 acres of open space including sixty–plus parks and 62 miles of multi-use trails. One of these parks, called Westerly Creek, is one of the largest in the area and offers access to some of the metro area's major regional trails, as well as a riparian greenway lush with an array of native trees, shrubs, grasses, and flowers that attract migratory birds and provide habitat for animals like beavers, foxes, and other small creatures. The Westerly Creek corridor is more than just a pleasant place for a stroll, it's an essential part of the area's entire ecosystem.

Locate the paved trail behind the covered picnic pavilion and turn right, heading south. You will quickly come to a road crossing, after which the trail descends toward a roundabout before meeting up with another road. Stay to the right, then turn left when you reach the street. (If you wish to add more mileage to your hike, feel free to continue straight across the street where the trail continues into the city of Aurora for several more miles. When you've seen enough, simply turn around and retrace your steps back to this point.) At the next corner, turn left to reenter the greenway; this time stay right around the circular path.

Now you are on the east side of the creek, where you have a beautiful view of the foothills stretched out to the west. After crossing back over Martin Luther King Jr. Boulevard, continue moving north on the main trail. On a hill to the right sits the Central

An old air traffic control tower anchors the Central Park neighborhood, which sits on the former site of Denver's original international airport.

Park Recreation Center, a top-notch fitness facility with an indoor pool, located in Central Park's "Eastbridge" community. On your left is a bridge where you'll cross the creek, gaining an elevated view of the area. This is a good spot to watch for raptors perched in a tree, or a beaver or muskrat scurrying through the gentle current. Continue heading north as the trail winds its way through a vast meadow of prairie grasses, shrubs, and small clumps of aspen and pine trees.

At the north end of the park, turn left and follow the trail around the corner until you are heading south again. Look west and you'll see the abandoned air traffic control tower presiding over Central Park, the neighborhood's namesake greenspace. You'll also get an up-close look at some neighborhood homes, which include a mix of classic foursquare, modern, and Victorian styles. Continue on this path until you reenter the trailhead on your right.

MILES AND DIRECTIONS

0.0 Locate the trail east of the parking lot, behind the picnic pavilion. Turn right to start the loop, moving south along the west side of the greenway.

0.05 Cross the road and continue straight.

0.23 Follow the trail around the west side of the roundabout.

Westerly Creek Park follows a riparian corridor rich with plant and animal life providing lush surroundings for recreationists.

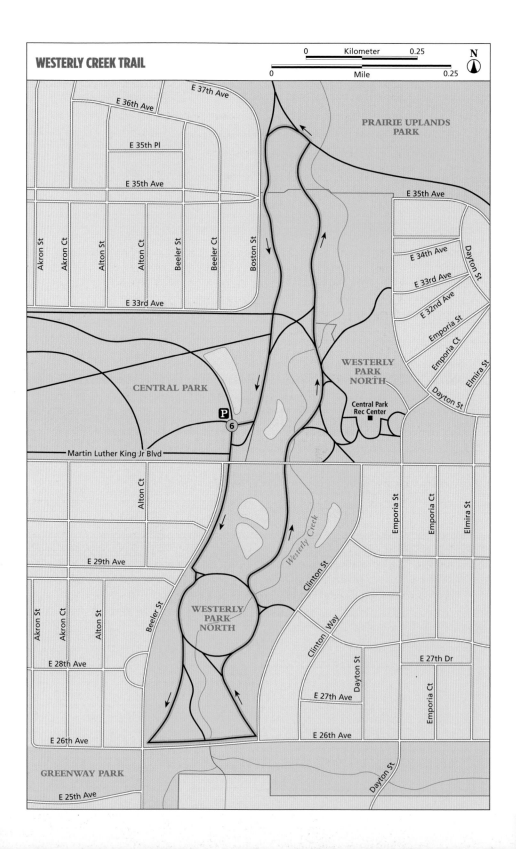

0.36 Stay right on the path leading up to the street.

0.47 Turn left at East 26th Avenue.

0.62 Turn left at the corner of East 26th Avenue and Clinton Street to reenter the greenway, heading north.

0.72 Stay right to move around the east side of the roundabout.

0.87 Follow the trail to the right, toward the east side of the creek.

1.1 Stay left toward the bridge. After crossing the creek, stay right.

1.5 Follow the trail to the left, around the northern end of the park.

2.0 Arrive back at the trailhead.

LOCAL INTEREST

Stanley Marketplace: This hip artisan outpost provides space for a variety of local vendors, including (but not limited to) bars, restaurants, fitness studios, and a handful of boutiques. It's a perfect one-stop shop for anything you need, including picnic supplies. 2501 N. Dallas St., Aurora; (720) 990-6743; stanleymarketplace.com

Lowry Beer Garden: If you're in need of some shade and an ice cold beverage after your hike, head to this breezy, low-key, Oktoberfest-style spot featuring a full bar, food menu, and 9,000-square-foot patio. 7577 E. Academy Blvd., Denver; (303) 366-0114; lowrybeergarden.com

Wings Over the Rockies Air & Space Museum: Located on a former Air Force base and rated as one of the top aviation museums in the world, you could spend hours exploring its collection of commercial and military aircraft and rotating exhibits. 7711 E. Academy Blvd., Denver; (303) 360-5360; wingsmuseum.org

LODGING

DoubleTree by Hilton Hotel Denver: Just blocks from the park, this property features modern, renovated rooms, three on-site restaurants, and an indoor pool. 3203 Quebec St., Denver; (303) 321-3333; hilton.com/en/hotels/rldv-dt-doubletree-denver

Beautiful Home in Charming Location (Airbnb): Live like a local in one of Denver's hottest residential areas in this spacious yet cozy suburban gem with three bedrooms, an outdoor patio, and a fireplace, located just blocks from Westerly Creek Park. airbnb.com/rooms/676825?federated_search_id=007965d3-47ee-4874-8f0b-bc732a 5bd07a&source_impression_id=p3_1615683980_AjWQmsNgBHbzgwbm&guests=1& adults=1

7 BLUFF LAKE LOOP

This short walk around the Bluff Lake Nature Center is a delight for families with children as well as nature-curious adults of all ages thanks to an emphasis on educational programming and discovery.

Elevation gain: 64 feet
Distance: 1.2-mile lollipop loop
Hiking time: About 1 hour
Difficulty: Moderate, due to slightly uneven terrain
Seasons: Year-round
Trail surface: Dirt
Land status: Bluff Lake Nature Center
City/Neighborhood: Denver (Central Park neighborhood)
Other trail users: None

Water availability: Yes, at trailhead
Canine compatibility: No dogs allowed
Fees and permits: None
Map: Bluff Lake Nature Center Map of Hiking Trails: blufflake.org/wp-content/uploads/2019/04/BLNC-Trails-Map.pdf
Trail contact: Bluff Lake Nature Center: (720) 708-4147
Trailhead GPS: N39 45.50' / E104 51.44'

FINDING THE TRAILHEAD

From downtown Denver, head east on 17th Avenue for about 2.5 miles. Turn left on Colorado Boulevard. In 1.2 miles turn right onto Martin Luther King Jr Boulevard. You'll see the entrance to Bluff Lake Nature Center on your left in 4.5 miles. (Bluff Lake Nature Center: 11255 MLK Jr. Blvd., Denver)

WHAT TO SEE

This hike is a true diamond in the rough—the land was obtained by the current management in a lawsuit involving the improper management of chemical runoff after the nearby Stapleton Airport closed in 1994, and is now a beautiful, peaceful 123-acre open space featuring several different environmental habitats and thriving with hundreds of species of plants and animals. Although it's little more than 1 mile in length, be sure to plan on spending at least 1 hour for your hike to allow time to watch for wildlife and interact with the numerous educational activities offered (printed bird-watching lists and "I Spy" brochures are provided at the trailhead). For an even more in-depth experience, you can also download/print the organization's self-guided tour booklet from the Bluff Lake Nature Center website (there are two—one for kids and one for adults).

Begin by walking toward the southwest corner of the parking lot, where you'll find a pergola offering views of downtown Denver and the foothills, as well as interpretive signboards with information about the various flora and fauna you will encounter on your hike. You can choose to take either the stairs or the ramp to access the trail below, making your way north. Turn left at the amphitheater to begin the loop, moving counterclockwise around the lake. Here the path is wide and serene, with ample shade provided by a corridor of cottonwood and aspen trees (both of which showcase brilliant yellow leaves in the fall). You'll also find some benches and birdhouses, making this a fine place to sit and take in the surroundings, even though you're just starting out. Keep your eyes peeled for signs of deer, foxes, and coyotes in this area.

This urban oasis houses a variety of wildlife ecosystems close to downtown.

You'll soon come to a narrow footpath on your right, which leads to a short loop around a meadow of prairie grasses, meeting back up with the main trail in less than one-quarter mile (the loop itself is about one-third mile). Feel free to explore this jaunt for a little extra mileage, or continue straight to stay on the main trail. Another optional spur is up ahead on your left—a wooden boardwalk that offers a closer look at the wetlands area on the southeast side of Bluff Lake. In this freshwater marsh it is likely you will spot abundant wildlife, cattails, various waterfowl, and signs of beaver activity, depending on the season. If you opted to take the additional loop trail, you can still access this boardwalk by turning left when you arrive back on the main trail and slightly backtracking southeast.

Continue along the main trail flanking the north side of the lake, along a riparian corridor and through a tunnel of willow trees, until you come to a bird blind, designed to allow for an incognito viewing opportunity. Due in part to its proximity to Sand Creek, which runs through the northeast section of the property, the Bluff Lake area is home to some 140 species of birds (although as many as 203 species have been spotted, as noted on the bird checklist provided at the trailhead), and this is one of the best places to stop, watch, and listen.

After the bird blind, the trail turns southeast up a gradual hill running parallel to Havana Street. The landscape looks much different now, as you have entered a shortgrass prairie zone. Here you might see prairie dogs and cottontail rabbits bobbing in and out between yucca and cactus plants. Notice that the bird boxes look a little different here, too. That is because they are actually bat boxes, which provide shelter for hundreds (hundreds!) of brown bats that help keep the mosquito population under control.

Sun-drenched trails are often accessible year-round, even after a snowfall.

Now you are on the homestretch of your hike. After passing the cattail–clogged catch basin at the southeastern corner of the lake and wetlands area, the trail turns north, leading you back to the amphitheater, where you can ascend the stairs (or ramp) back to the parking area.

Close encounters with wildlife, such as this coyote, are common here.

MILES AND DIRECTIONS

0.0 Begin at the pergola structure at the southwest corner of the parking area. You can take either the stairs or the ramp to access the trail below the bluff.

0.1 The amphitheater marks the beginning of the main loop.

0.17 At the intersection, continue straight to stay on the main trail. Or turn right to add on the optional 0.3-mile meadow loop.

0.3 Turn left down a 0.05-mile boardwalk to access a wetlands viewing platform. Retrace your steps back to the main trail.

0.31 Stay left to continue on the main trail.

0.56 Round the corner at the bird blind structure and continue southeast along the trail.

0.88 Stay left on the trail.

1.1 Arrive back at the amphitheater. Turn right and ascend the stairs/ramp back toward the parking lot.

1.3 Arrive back at the parking lot.

LOCAL INTEREST

Eastbridge Town Center: Located in the Central Park neighborhood bordering the nature center, this small collection of boutique stores and locally owned restaurants offers

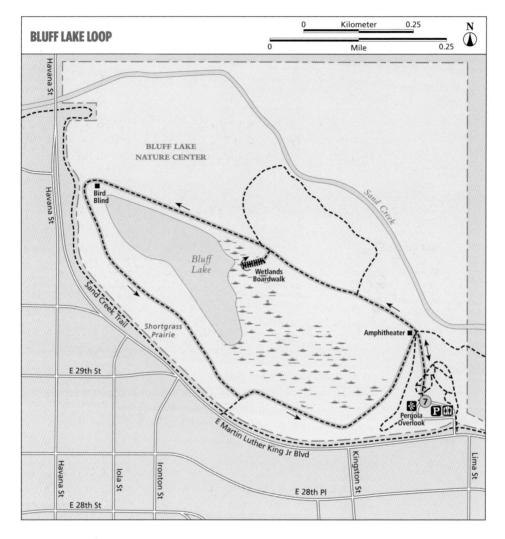

a great off-the-beaten-path spot to relax and refuel. 10155 E. 29th Dr.; eastbridgetown
center.com

Central Park Outdoor Markets: The nearby Central Park community offers a robust
schedule of seasonal events like festivals, farmers' markets, movies, and block parties.
Check the online calendar for details. denver80238.com/whats-happening

LODGING

Embassy Suites by Hilton Denver Central Park: Simple yet modern accommodations with an indoor pool, room service, and on-site restaurant and bar that offers a
complimentary happy hour reception daily. Located just minutes north of Bluff Lake
Nature Center. 4444 N. Havana St., Denver; (303) 375-0400; hilton.com/en/hotels/
denares-embassy-suites-denver-central-park

8 CHERRY CREEK TRAIL— CHERRY CREEK MALL TO CHERRY CREEK STATE PARK

This section of one of Denver's most iconic trails meanders along a pretty stream from city to suburbs, offering a tour of southeastern Denver neighborhoods, each with its own amenities, history, and scenery.

Elevation gain: 225 feet
Distance: 13.5 miles out and back
Hiking time: About 4 hours
Difficulty: Easy
Seasons: Year-round
Trail surface: Paved
Land status: City and County of Denver
Nearest town: Denver, Glendale (Cherry Creek neighborhood)
Other trail users: Cyclists, joggers

Water availability: No
Canine compatibility: Yes, on leash
Fees and permits: None
Map: Denver Bike Map: denvergov .org/content/dam/denvergov/ Portals/708/documents/2017 -Denver-Bike-Map.pdf
Trail contact: Denver Parks & Recreation: (720) 913-1311
Trailhead GPS: N39 42.77' / E104 56.81'

FINDING THE TRAILHEAD

From downtown Denver, drive south on Speer Boulevard. In about 3 miles, stay right onto Steele Street as the road splits, then turn left on East Bayaud Avenue. Turn right on Madison Street, then right into the parking area.

WHAT TO SEE

This section of the 40-mile Cherry Creek regional trail—which was built along the remains of the Cherokee Trail, an original wagon route used by homesteaders and gold miners—starts in the heart of the upscale Cherry Creek neighborhood, a popular shopping and dining destination, and ends near Cherry Creek State Park in Aurora. As the trail travels from a bustling commercial district southeast through suburban residential areas, the landscape becomes more spacious, inviting wildlife and vegetation to thrive, creating a pleasant atmosphere for people to enjoy, too. In addition to wildlife and natural scenery, the trail passes by a variety of parks and open spaces, each with their own amenities, histories, and curiosities. The parks also offer nice places to take breaks, or can be used as alternative access points, as this trail is on the longer side.

Start out walking southeast on the trail, with the creek on your right-hand side. The main trail is paved, but you'll also notice that several dirt "social" paths have been carved along the side of the creek that you're welcome to explore, too. The path—commonly referred to as the Cherry Creek bike path—is often busy with joggers, dog walkers, and cyclists of all kinds, especially where it intersects with the High Line Canal Trail, as both are heavily utilized by bike commuters. As such, be sure to stay to the right and yield to other trail users as necessary.

This section of trail is situated alongside Cherry Creek, dividing the busy Cherry Creek Drive thoroughfare into north and south routes, acting as a sort of boulevard. Right away the trail will pass through a small green space dedicated to two of Denver's ten sister cities. On the north side of the trail, the tiny Takayama Park features a rock garden with bonsai-like trees to honor its Japanese heritage. The city of Brest (France) Park, located on the south side of the trail, is larger, with a variety of park benches and picnic tables, frequently used by local office workers seeking fresh air on their lunch breaks.

It becomes much quieter after Colorado Boulevard, where the busy streets move away from the trail, the high-rise buildings fade from sight, and the creek corridor becomes wider. Soon you'll come upon the Four Mile Historic Park, the site of Denver's oldest house and a wonderful cultural offering, especially for families with children. For a small entrance fee you can tour 12 acres of nature trails, pan for "gold," visit farm animals, and browse the museum to learn more about early western settlements. The restroom and picnic facilities also make this a nice break spot.

After a long straightaway that transports you through the city of Glendale—a home-rule municipality best known for its rugby stadium and training center—you'll come to another series of parks: the city of Potenza Park, another commemorative sister city space; Garland Park, a large recreation area with a playground, lake, and ball fields; and Cook Park, housing a recreation center and outdoor pool. After passing these parks, the trail moves deeper into more quiet residential zones as it creeps away from the dense city.

Both the trail and creek become wider and more lush as they travel away from the city and move toward Cherry Creek State Park.

The scenery along the trail is lush and lovely, with a variety of mature trees offering shade and aesthetic interest.

Here the creek becomes wider and moves more slowly, attracting ducks and other water-fowl to its greenish brown pools flanked by rows of cottonwood trees. Prairie plants such as rabbitbrush, yucca, and cactus grow alongside the trail, which curves under and around roadways every mile or so. Be sure to follow signage and use crosswalk signals as directed to safely navigate road crossings—especially around the intersection with the High Line Canal Trail, where there are several twists and turns and interchanges.

You'll pass a trailhead at Wabash Street as well as the back side of the Cherry Creek Country Club—giving you a glimpse into the cavernous homes of Denver's rich and famous—before reaching the Kennedy Golf Course, signaling your homestretch. Here the trail becomes surprisingly hilly, but the climb is worth it as you'll be rewarded with panoramic views of the foothills and city skyline when you reach the top. When you find yourself at the top of the golf course, across from the ball fields—where there are a hand-ful of park benches to help you comfortably take in the views—you have reached the turnaround point and may now retrace your steps back to the parking area, or continue on for many more miles of hiking as the trail passes through Cherry Creek State Park (located to the south, beyond the highway and the looming wall of the reservoir dam) and through the suburban city of Parker before ending in Franktown, near Castlewood Canyon State Park.

MILES AND DIRECTIONS

0.0 Walk south from the parking lot toward East Alameda Avenue. Cross the intersec-tion to access the trail, then turn left to begin hiking southeast, with the creek on your right.

1.7 Stay right to continue on the main trail.

5.1 Stay left and follow signs for the Cherry Creek Trail.

5.2 Stay right and follow signs for the Cherry Creek Trail.

5.3 Stay left and follow signs for the Cherry Creek Trail.

5.8 Continue straight.

6.0 Stay right.

6.7 At the top of the hill across from John F. Kennedy Ballfields, turn around and retrace your steps back to the trailhead.

13.5 Arrive back at Pulaski Park.

LOCAL INTEREST

Bull and Bush Brewery: This cozy English-style pub has been around since the 1970s and remains one of the most revered breweries in the Denver area. In addition to their own craft brand, they also feature an array of beers from around the world, as well as a full bar and food menu. 4700 E. Cherry Creek South Dr., Glendale; (303) 759-0333; bullandbush.com

Cherry Creek North: Located a few blocks from the massive Cherry Creek Shop-ping Center, this charming outdoor "mall" is filled with chic boutiques, art galleries, restaurants, cafes, yoga studios, and day spas. During the summer it often hosts events like live music performances and art shows. 2401 E. 2nd Ave., Denver; (303) 394-2904; cherrycreeknorth.com

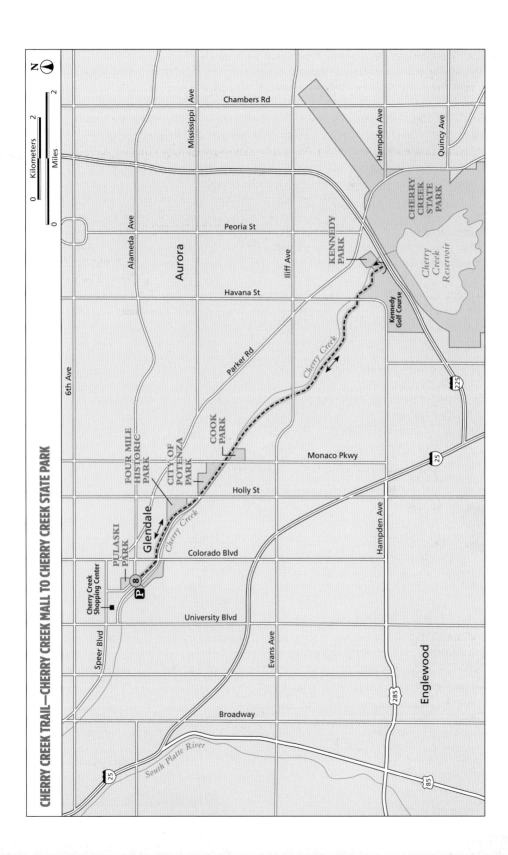

CHERRY CREEK TRAIL—CHERRY CREEK MALL TO CHERRY CREEK STATE PARK

N

0   Kilometers   2

0   Miles   2

Chambers Rd

Mississippi Ave

Hampden Ave

Quincy Ave

CHERRY CREEK STATE PARK

Cherry Creek Reservoir

Alameda Ave

Peoria St

Aurora

Iliff Ave

KENNEDY PARK

Havana St

Kennedy Golf Course

6th Ave

Parker Rd

Cherry Creek

225

FOUR MILE HISTORIC PARK

CITY OF POTENZA PARK

COOK PARK

Monaco Pkwy

25

Glendale

Holly St

Cherry Creek

PULASKI PARK

Colorado Blvd

Hampden Ave

Cherry Creek Shopping Center

P 8

University Blvd

Speer Blvd

Evans Ave

Englewood

285

Broadway

25

South Platte River

85

The Cherry Cricket: A visit to this retro Denver dive bar for an award-winning burger (featured on the Travel Channel's *Man vs. Food*) and a beer on the patio is a must. 2641 E. 2nd Ave. Denver; (303) 322-7666; cherrycricket.com

Cherry Creek Fresh Market: Don't miss the colorful array of local produce, artisan goods, food truck vendors, and people that flock to the shopping center parking lot on Wednesday and Saturday mornings in the summertime. 1st Avenue and University Boulevard, Denver; (303) 442-1837; coloradofreshmarkets.com/home

LODGING

Staybridge Suites Denver-Cherry Creek: Offering direct access to Cherry Creek and the trail, this hotel makes you feel right at home with pet-friendly rooms featuring fully equipped kitchens, an outdoor pool, and complimentary transportation. 4220 E.Virginia Ave., Glendale; (303) 321-5757; ihg.com/staybridge/hotels/us/en/glendale/dench/hoteldetail

Cherry Creek State Park: Scenic, well-maintained campgrounds with shower and laundry facilities are available year-round for tents and RVs, offering direct access to trails for hiking, biking, and horseback riding and a reservoir for boating, paddling, and fishing. 4201 S. Parker Rd., Aurora; (800) 244-5613; cpw.state.co.us/buyapply/Pages/Reservations.aspx

Halcyon Hotel Cherry Creek: Located in Cherry Creek North, this modern boutique hotel aims to impress with its rooftop pool, complimentary "gear garage," and chic on-site eatery. 245 Columbine St., Denver; (720) 772-5000; halcyonhotelcherrycreek.com

9 **WASHINGTON PARK OUTER LOOP**

This loop around one of Denver's most cherished neighborhood parks is the perfect length for a quick jog or stroll—just make sure you leave extra time to stop and smell the flowers, or have a picnic by the lake.

Elevation gain: 24 feet
Distance: 2.5-mile loop
Hiking time: About 1 hour
Difficulty: Easy
Seasons: Year-round
Trail surface: Paved, dirt
Land status: City of Denver
Nearest town: Denver (Wash Park neighborhood)
Other trail users: Cyclists
Water availability: Yes

Canine compatibility: Yes, on leash
Fees and permits: None
Map: City of Denver Map of Washington Park Trails: denvergov .org/files/assets/public/parks -and-recreation/documents/trails/ washington_park_loops.pdf
Trail contact: Denver Parks and Recreation: (720) 913-1311
Trailhead GPS: N39 42.25' / E104 58.36'

FINDING THE TRAILHEAD

From downtown Denver, drive east on Speer Boulevard for about 1 mile, then turn right on North Downing Street. In about 1 more mile, turn left into the park at the traffic light at Exposition Avenue. The parking area is on your left.

WHAT TO SEE

The name Washington Park—best known as simply "Wash" Park—pertains to both a residential neighborhood and the 150-plus-acre green space located at its core, both of which are heralded for their scenic beauty, friendliness, and sense of community. The park itself is one of the city's most popular destinations for recreation, with meadows dotted with mature trees, well-maintained hard- and soft-surface trails, and picture-perfect lakes. Developed in the Victorian era, the park features two lakes, several formal flower gardens (rumored to resemble those of George Washington's Mount Vernon home), and a historic boathouse. Modern additions include a recreation center and numerous sports courts and playgrounds. The Outer Loop trail encircles the entire property, offering beautiful scenery, excellent people watching, and a tour of residential architecture, but exploring the inner trails that hug the lake and poke around the gardens is also recommended, as these are often less populated and offer surprises like lovely gardens and shady benches.

Starting from the parking area near the southwest corner of Smith Lake, walk west across the inner road and look for the crushed gravel path running parallel to South Downing Street. Turn right on this path to begin hiking north, moving clockwise around the park. Smith Lake will quickly come into full view, as will the historic Dos Chappell Bathhouse, which in its early days was used as a warming hut for ice skating in the winter, and a swimming pavilion where swimsuits, towels, and lockers were available for rent in the summer. While swimming and ice skating are no longer permitted on the lake, it is still a popular place for pedal boats and fishing.

If you're lucky, you might discover a historic boathouse at the end of the rainbow.

Continue around the corner to the right, moving east along East Virginia Avenue. The path ascends a small hill and winds around a cluster of picnic tables near a small fishing pond before rounding another corner. In the winter, bald eagles often come to nest in the tall cottonwood trees on this eastern bank, the more remote area of the park. When the trail emerges into the open again, you have a great view of the boathouse across the lake, whose lights reflect off the water at night, revealing a romantic ambience for evening strolls.

Now, moving south on a long straightaway along South Franklin Street, you will get a personal parade of homes—many of which represent the classic Craftsman-style bungalows the neighborhood is known for—and some are quite grand. Behind the boathouse sits the Washington Park Recreation Center, where an indoor pool was constructed in 1971 following the closure of the Smith Lake swimming beach. The path here is wide and smooth, following a slight hill, and is usually crowded with people jogging and walking dogs. The field to your right is the largest in the city's extensive park system, and is a very popular place for volleyball leagues, picnics, and sunbathing. Travel six blocks down any of the side streets on your left and you'll happen upon South Gaylord Street, a quaint collection of boutiques, bakeries, breweries, and restaurants, surrounded by more magnificent homes.

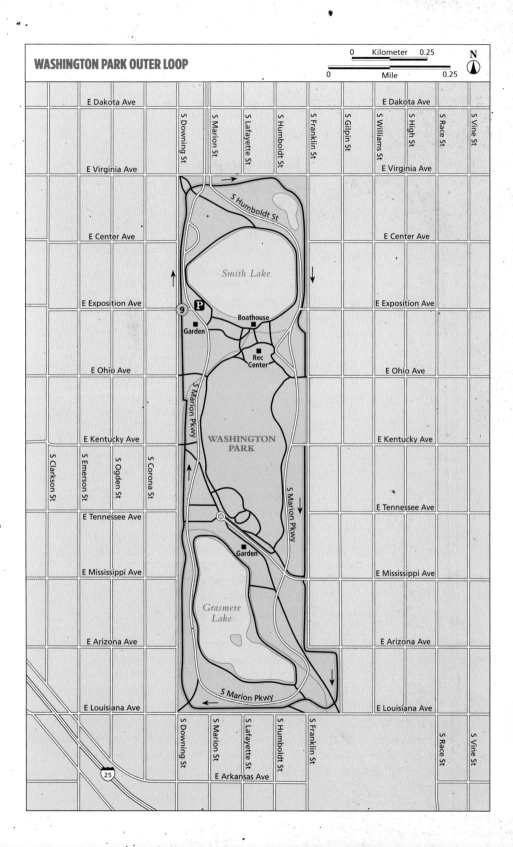

WASHINGTON PARK OUTER LOOP

Kilometer 0.25
Mile 0.25

N

E Dakota Ave

S Downing St
S Marion St
S Lafayette St
S Humboldt St
S Franklin St
S Gilpin St
S Williams St
S High St
S Race St
S Vine St

E Dakota Ave

E Virginia Ave

E Virginia Ave

S Humboldt St

E Center Ave

E Center Ave

Smith Lake

E Exposition Ave

9

P

E Exposition Ave

Boathouse

Garden

Rec Center

E Ohio Ave

E Ohio Ave

S Marion Pkwy

E Kentucky Ave

WASHINGTON PARK

E Kentucky Ave

S Clarkson St
S Emerson St
S Ogden St
S Corona St

S Marion Pkwy

E Tennessee Ave

E Tennessee Ave

Garden

E Mississippi Ave

E Mississippi Ave

Grasmere Lake

E Arizona Ave

E Arizona Ave

S Marion Pkwy

E Louisiana Ave

E Louisiana Ave

S Downing St
S Marion St
S Lafayette St
S Humboldt St
S Franklin St
S Race St
S Vine St

25

E Arkansas Ave

A lawn bowling court and sculptured gardens on Grasmere Lake pay homage to its English namesake and Victorian roots.

When you reach Arizona Street, follow the path as it turns left around the southeast corner of the park, featuring an overview of Grasmere Lake with snowcapped mountains in the background. Taking a closer look at this man-made lake will reveal an array of wildlife sightings, including turtles, fish, muskrats, ducks, geese, pelicans, and more. It is well worth your time and energy to diverge from the main trail and venture down the narrow, paved path that hugs the water's edge, which will not only give you a better view of the wildlife, but also lead you to an amazing garden located on the north side of the lake. Another unique feature you'll come across near the garden is a historic lawn bowling green, where club groups still gather to play croquet and bocce ball.

As you round the next corner, continuing west, you'll cross over the historic "city ditch," which once diverted water from the South Platte River for irrigation. Here the trail passes through a tunnel of trees: oak, spruce, honeylocust, and maple shade the path and create a serene atmosphere. After rounding the corner at South Downing Street and

East Louisiana Avenue, you are on the homestretch—and a particularly lovely one at that. On this side of the park the trail is wide and flat, and travels down a corridor of massive honeylocust trees and past a beautiful maze of flower beds. This garden is well tended and changed out seasonally, displaying everything from roses in June to purple cabbage in October. Soon after passing the garden you will find yourself back at the trailhead parking area.

MILES AND DIRECTIONS

0.0 Cross the paved trail east of the parking lot and locate the dirt path, parallel to South Downing Street.

0.17 Stay left.

0.4 Follow the dirt path around the corner to the right.

0.92 Continue straight, across the driveway.

1.2 Continue straight, across the driveway.

1.3 Turn left to stay on the dirt trail.

1.5 Stay on the dirt path as it turns and heads west.

1.8 Continue around the corner, heading north.

2.3 Continue straight, across the driveway.

2.5 Arrive back at the parking area.

LOCAL INTEREST

South Pearl Street Farmers Market: On Sunday mornings in the summer this local main drag is closed to cars and packed full of produce stands, craft booths, food trucks, and sidewalk sales, offering prime people watching and bar/restaurant hopping. Intersection of South Pearl Street and Florida Avenue, Denver; (303) 734-0718; southpearlstreet.com/farmers-market

Bonnie Brae Ice Cream: In recent years Denver has been flooded with a bevy of hipster ice cream shops, but this retro parlor has been keeping it classic since the mid-1980s. The large menu board of old-fashioned, homemade flavors and the friendly customer service guarantee a line around the corner late into the evening. 799 S. University Blvd., Denver; (303) 777-0808; bonniebraeicecream.com

Vert Kitchen: Pick up the perfect gourmet picnic spread from this perky French cafe, to be enjoyed in nearby Wash Park or on its own charming outdoor patio. 704 S. Pearl St., Denver; (303) 997-5941; vertkitchen.com

Homegrown Tap & Dough: A friendly neighborhood pizza joint complete with a dog-friendly patio, lawn games, and a simple yet stellar Italian menu. 1001 S. Gaylord St., Denver; (720) 459-8736; tapanddough.com

LODGING

Courtyard Denver Cherry Creek: Friendly, comfortable property with an on-site coffee shop, bar, and outdoor patio. Ask for a west-facing room for an amazing view of the Rocky Mountains. 1475 S. Colorado Blvd., Denver; (303) 757-8797; marriott.com/hotels/travel/dench-courtyard-denver-cherry-creek

10 EAST HARVARD GULCH TRAIL

This nondescript path is a local favorite for residents looking for a quick and easy place to take the dog for a walk, go for a jog, ride bikes, and connect with nature away from the more well-known (read: crowded) park loops and regional trails.

Elevation gain: 88 feet
Distance: 5.3 miles out and back
Hiking time: About 2 hours
Difficulty: Easy
Seasons: Year-round
Trail surface: Paved
Land status: City and County of Denver
Nearest town: Denver (University neighborhood)
Other trail users: Joggers, cyclists
Water availability: Yes, at trailhead

Canine compatibility: Yes, on leash
Fees and permits: None
Map: City of Denver Map of Harvard Gulch Park: denvergov.org/content/dam/denvergov/Portals/747/documents/ParkArt/ParkArt_Harvard%20Gulch%20Park.pdf
Trail contact: Denver Parks and Recreation: (720) 913-1311
Trailhead GPS: N39 40.46' / E104 58.82'

FINDING THE TRAILHEAD

From downtown Denver, drive south on Broadway for about 4.5 miles. Turn left on East Iliff Avenue, then right into the parking area. (Harvard Gulch Park: 550 E. Iliff Ave., Denver)

WHAT TO SEE

This hike takes you on a journey through a series of quaint residential areas on the southern border of Denver proper via a patchwork of paths, alleys, and sidewalks, offering an intimate look at daily life in some of Denver's most sought-after neighborhoods. Home to the University of Denver campus, the surrounding areas offer an interesting mix of student housing and dive bars alongside stately homes and mature trees. The minimally maintained "trail" passes through several small parks and along the Harvard Gulch waterway providing urban habitat for birds, turtles, squirrels, and other small creatures that appreciate the peace and quiet of the understated route.

Begin by walking southeast through Harvard Gulch Park, located in the quiet Rosedale neighborhood. Although the Harvard Gulch is an important urban waterway, these days the name is most recognized as the laid-back yet lively par-three golf course on the south half of the park, which is often crowded with young people in shorts and sandals on sunny days. When you reach Harvard Avenue, turn left and walk east on the sidewalk until the trail resumes after crossing South Downing Street. Since the trail lies almost entirely within neighborhoods, plan to cross a lot of small streets. In most instances the trail is easily detectable, despite a few zigs and zags for crosswalks and such, but use your best judgment to guide you if the way-finding becomes a bit vague.

Facing page top: In addition to local residents, geese and other waterfowl are also attracted to the lush vegetation harbored along the trail.
Bottom: This route passes through several of Denver's most coveted neighborhoods and their respective local parks, which offer a nice change of scenery from the residential streets.

Now in the University region, the trail hugs the concrete ditch as it cuts through an expanse of lovely residential neighborhoods featuring many different types of trees, unassuming ranch-style homes, and nicely painted crosswalks for trail users (be prepared to cross a small street on every block). DeBoer Park offers a nice break from the frequent street crossings, with a playground, interpretive signage about the history of the area, and ample lawn areas. You'll soon reach University Boulevard, a busy thoroughfare that serves as a sort of "main drag" for the college district. You can easily see the trail across the road, but it's safer to cross at the intersection to the south, even if it adds a little mileage to your trek.

Once safely across University, you'll find yourself walking through the esteemed Observatory Park neighborhood (also referred to as University Park), which offers an array of cultural amenities like the Chamberlin Observatory and the University of Denver theater. A mix of home styles is also present, with the modest bungalows of old peppered with modern mansions thanks to a frenzy of developer scrapes in recent years. The trail travels through Robert H. McWilliams Park, featuring a playground popular with the neighborhood youngsters and a multitude of tree species including oak, spruce, pine, maple, and honeylocust.

The path takes on a few more wonky street crossings as it meanders through a residential area and a short greenway before coming to an abrupt end in a parking lot just before reaching Colorado Boulevard, one of Denver's busiest commercial roadways. Turn around here and follow the same route back to the trailhead at Harvard Gulch Park.

MILES AND DIRECTIONS

0.0 Locate the trail southeast of the parking lot and begin walking east.

0.13 Turn right and continue moving southeast.

0.3 Turn left and walk down the sidewalk along East Harvard Avenue.

0.44 Cross South Downing Street and locate the footpath.

0.5 Continue straight, across South Marion Street.

0.57 Continue straight, across South Lafayette Street.

0.64 Continue straight, across South Humboldt Street.

0.7 Continue straight, across South Franklin Street.

0.76 Continue straight, across South Gilpin Street.

0.83 Continue straight, across South Williams Street.

0.9 Continue straight, taking a slight jog to the right across South High Street.

1.0 Continue straight, across South Race Street, entering DeBoer Park.

1.1 Turn right, across the bridge.

1.2 Turn right on South York Street and look for the path to resume on your left.

1.3 At South University Boulevard, turn right and walk south to use the crosswalk at the intersection of Yale Avenue. Once safely on the east side of the road, turn left and walk north back up University.

1.5 Turn right to rejoin the trail, heading east.

1.6 Continue straight, taking a slight jog to the left across South Josephine Street.

1.7 Continue straight, taking a slight jog to the right across South Columbine Street into Robert H. McWilliams Park.

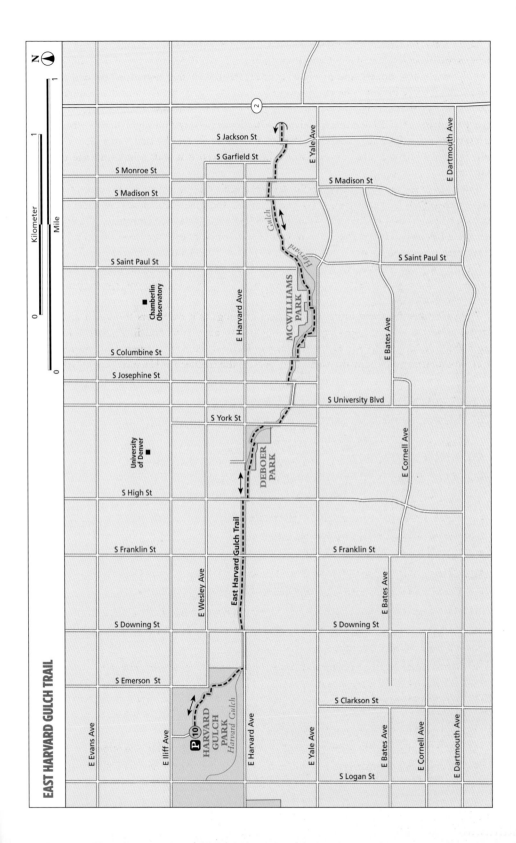

EAST HARVARD GULCH TRAIL

N

Kilometer
Mile

S Jackson St
S Garfield St
S Monroe St
S Madison St
E Yale Ave
S Madison St
E Dartmouth Ave
S Saint Paul St
Gulch
Harvard
S Saint Paul St
Chamberlin Observatory
E Harvard Ave
MCWILLIAMS PARK
E Bates Ave
S Columbine St
S Josephine St
S University Blvd
S York St
E Cornell Ave
University of Denver
DEBOER PARK
S High St
S Franklin St
East Harvard Gulch Trail
S Franklin St
E Wesley Ave
E Bates Ave
S Downing St
S Downing St
E Evans Ave
S Emerson St
S Clarkson St
E Iliff Ave
HARVARD GULCH PARK
Harvard Gulch
E Harvard Ave
E Yale Ave
E Bates Ave
E Cornell Ave
E Dartmouth Ave
S Logan St

1.9	Follow the path as it jogs left, then right, continuing northeast through the green space.
2.2	Cross diagonally at the intersection of East Vassar Avenue and South Adams Street, moving northeast.
2.25	Continue straight, across South Cook Street.
2.3	Continue straight, taking a slight jog to the left across South Madison Street.
2.4	Continue straight, taking a slight jog to the right across South Monroe Street.
2.5	Continue straight, taking a slight jog to the left across South Jackson Street.
2.6	The trail will dead-end in a retail parking lot near Colorado Boulevard. Turn around and retrace your steps back to the trailhead.
5.3	Arrive back at Harvard Gulch Park.

LOCAL INTEREST

Roaming Buffalo Bar-B-Que: Get to this hole-in-the-wall "craft" barbecue joint before they sell out of the daily specials, which can be anything from "brisket burnt ends" to "smoked and loaded spuds," and don't be afraid to try adventurous items like venison sausage and pulled Colorado lamb (served by the pound!). 2387 S. Downing St., Denver; (303) 722-2226; roamingbuffalobbq.com/denver

The Pioneer: Lovingly referred to as simply the "Pie-Oh," this is one of the most hoppin' bars in the small college town, with regulars of all ages bellying up for the twice-per-day happy hour specials, and to celebrate the namesake sports team of the nearby University of Denver. A menu of tacos and wings is available to help soak up the booze. 2401 S. University Blvd., Denver; (720) 536-4802; thepioneerbar.com

LODGING

La Quinta Inn by Wyndham Denver Cherry Creek: Modest yet sufficient accommodations in the University of Denver area, with an outdoor pool and proximity to an array of basic restaurants, shops, and conveniences. 1975 S. Colorado Blvd., Denver; (303) 758-8886; wyndhamhotels.com/laquinta/denver-colorado/la-quinta-inn-denver-cherry-creek/overview

11 RUBY HILL PARK LOOP

Head to this park for amazing views of the downtown city skyline and epic people-watching opportunities, thanks to a variety of community amenities like a concert venue, outdoor pool, and an innovative terrain park for bikers and skiers.

Elevation gain: 117 feet
Distance: 1.5-mile loop
Hiking time: About 30 minutes
Difficulty: Moderate
Seasons: Year-round
Trail surface: Dirt
Land status: City and County of Denver
Nearest town: Denver (Ruby Hill neighborhood)
Other trail users: Mountain bikers
Water availability: Yes, at trailhead

Canine compatibility: Yes, on leash
Fees and permits: None
Map: Denver Parks & Recreation Ruby Hill Park Map: denvergov
.org/content/dam/denvergov/
Portals/747/documents/ParkArt/
ParkArt_Ruby%20Hill%20Park.pdf
Trail contact: Denver Parks & Recreation: (720) 913-1311
Trailhead GPS: N39 40.95' / E105 00.25'

FINDING THE TRAILHEAD

From downtown Denver, take Broadway south for about 3 miles. Turn right on West Mississippi Avenue, then left on South Platte River Drive. Turn right on Jewell Avenue in about 1 mile, then right into the parking lot by the baseball fields.

WHAT TO SEE

Located about 5 miles south of downtown Denver, Ruby Hill Park is an urban redevelopment success story: What was once a landfill is now an especially entertaining place to recreate thanks to an array of amenities that attract people from all over the city. In addition to playgrounds, a public pool, and a variety of ball fields, Ruby Hill is home to a unique terrain park for biking and skating in the summer, and skiing and snowboarding in the winter. Sledding is also a favorite pastime here, as the park offers some of the hilliest terrain in the metro area. A multi-use dirt path encircles the entire park, offering a somewhat rugged hiking experience. And while most other trails in the Denver area are popular for their views of the mountains, Ruby Hill is one of the only places where you can find a good view of the city itself.

Starting on the west side of the park along Jewell Avenue, begin walking north around the bike park. Right away you'll understand where the park gets its name, as the trail climbs up a somewhat steep hill and curves around the terrain park, where you can marvel at the daredevils practicing their mountain biking and skiing/snowboarding skills by jumping off ramps, zooming around corners, and sliding down rails. The trail continues gradually uphill as you approach the playground and pool area. The Ruby Hill Community Garden is also located here, where neighbors work together to learn growing techniques, maintain seasonal plots, and share the bounty of their crops. Continue north on the outermost path until it rounds a corner, turning east. Here the path splits, and you'll stay right to ascend yet another hill. On the way to the top, the trail travels up through

This top-notch terrain park attracts mountain bikers, skiers, and snowboarders to challenge themselves with a variety of obstacles.

Offering a nice mix of urban amenities and natural habitat, this is a lovely place to watch the sunset.

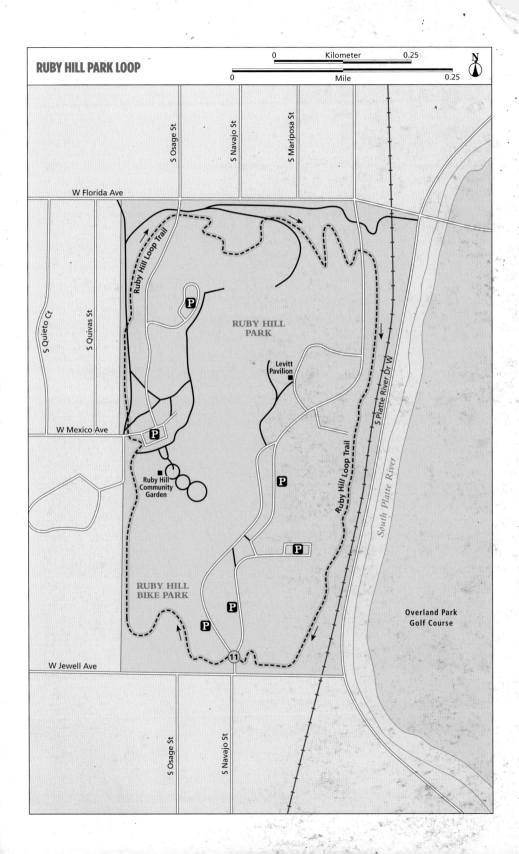

a pretty grove of trees and alongside an impressive picnic pavilion before delivering you to an open area where you are awarded with 360-degree views. With the mountains to the west, the South Platte River to the east, and the city skyline to the north, this is a wonderful place to watch the sunset.

After taking in the view, and perhaps a few photos, relocate the trail on the northeast side of the hill and begin your descent. At the bottom, continue along the dirt path as it turns right and heads south along South Platte River Drive. Here you'll notice a road leading to a structure known as the Levitt Pavilion, where outdoor concerts are held in the summer (many of which are free to attend) and people sprawl out on the expansive, grassy lawn behind the stage. As the trail ambles its way around the southeast corner of the park, be mindful of sharing the narrowing trail with an abundance of mountain bikers as you approach the bike park and return to the trailhead parking area.

MILES AND DIRECTIONS

0.0 Locate the trail on the northwest corner of the parking lot and begin hiking north, moving clockwise around the park.

0.4 Continue straight on the outermost path, moving north.

0.67 Stay right to ascend the hill.

0.98 Follow the path as it turns right and heads south along South Platte River Drive.

1.5 Arrive back at the parking lot.

LOCAL INTEREST

Maria Empanada: A cheerful Latin kitchen specializing in traditional Argentine pastries stuffed with a variety of sweet and savory fillings. Try a few different flavors with a pitcher of sangria on the outdoor patio. 1298 S. Broadway Ave., Denver; (303) 934-2221; mariaempanada.com

The Post Chicken and Beer: Don't miss this home-style Southern spot featuring juicy fried chicken, gooey mac and cheese, and craft beer on tap, plus a brunch menu and outdoor patio to boot. 2200 S. Broadway Ave., Denver; (720) 466-5699; postbrewing .com/rosedale

LODGING

La Quinta Inn Denver Cherry Creek: Basic accommodations in a central location, featuring an outdoor pool and free breakfast. 1975 S. Colorado Blvd., Denver; (303) 758-8886; wyndhamhotels.com/laquinta/denver-colorado/la-quinta-inn-denver-cherry-creek/ overview?CID=LC:LQ::GGL:RIO:National:52670&iata=00093796

NORTH METRO

The cities located just north of Denver are often brushed off as solely industrial zones full of factories and freeways, but there are some true treasures to be found here in the way of outdoor recreation. In addition to a variety of creekside trail systems that pass through the region—which provide commuter connectivity, neighborhood nature access, and wildlife corridors—it is home to several major conservation areas, including not one but *two* national wildlife refuges. And serious bird watchers and wildlife photographers flock from across the state to Barr Lake State Park, which contains some of the best bald eagle nesting habitat around.

Also included in this section is the northwest city of Arvada, a charming town boasting an array of historic, cultural, and entertainment attractions that will satisfy urban urges. Among its quiet, suburban residential streets runs Ralston Creek—the city's most celebrated geological feature. A number of parks, trails, and landmarks have been developed along its banks—several of which you'll soon read about in the following pages—offering endless exploration and enjoyment for both residents and visitors alike.

A landscape of juxtaposing features, from wetlands to smokestacks.

Surrounded on all sides by warehouses, highways, and homes, the 14-mile Sand Creek Greenway bisects the north Denver region, offering a much-needed urban respite for both humans and wildlife.

12 SAND CREEK GREENWAY— DAHLIA TRAILHEAD TO HAVANA STREET

Experience how even the smallest slivers of water and vegetation can breathe life into urban environments on this section of a 14-mile commuter route that offers plants, animals, and people a much-needed brush with nature through some of the metro area's busiest commercial zones.

Elevation gain: 125 feet
Distance: 10.0 miles out and back
Hiking time: About 3 hours
Difficulty: Easy
Seasons: Year-round
Trail surface: Paved, dirt, sand
Land status: City of Commerce City, City and County of Denver
Nearest town: Commerce City, Denver
Other trail users: Cyclists, equestrians

Water availability: No
Canine compatibility: Yes, on leash
Fees and permits: None
Map: Sand Creek Regional Greenway Trail Map: americantrails.org/files/pdf/SandCreek-NRT-map.pdf
Trail contact: Sand Creek Regional Greenway Partnership: (303) 468-3263
Trailhead GPS: N39 47.84' / E104 55.83'

FINDING THE TRAILHEAD

From downtown Denver, take I-25 North to exit 214A for I-70 East. Then, take exit 276A onto US 6 East toward Vasquez Boulevard and turn left onto Steele Street. In about 1.5 miles, turn right on East 56th Avenue, then right on Sand-creek Drive. The parking area is on your right. (Dahlia Trailhead: 4900 Sandcreek Dr. S., Denver)

WHAT TO SEE

The Sand Creek Regional Greenway is one of Denver's premier connector trails, spanning about 14 miles across the northern metro area between the South Platte River Trail in the west, and the High Line Canal Trail in the east, creating an impressive urban trail network for both pedestrian and bike commuters. The greenway provides access to a multitude of residential neighborhoods, parks, conservation areas, and educational facilities along the way. This section of the trail runs parallel to the I-270 and I-70 freeways, hugging the banks of Sand Creek, a narrow wetland and riparian habitat that provides habitat for wildlife and vegetation in the midst of a concrete jungle (see the Bluff Lake Loop and Star K Ranch Double Loop hikes to learn more about other sections of the Sand Creek Greenway).

Begin hiking southeast on the paved trail, with the creek on your right-hand side. The first few miles of the path are located in Commerce City, where warehouses and factories loom over the creek, and smokestacks and busy streets dominate the surrounding environment. The Sand Creek Regional Greenway Partnership, a nonprofit organization that manages stewardship and education of the trail, has done a good job of securing

A beautiful mural, painted by local artist Yulia Avgustinovich (yulia-art.com), brightens up a concrete wall.

Can you spot the tumbleweed stuck in this city-meets-nature landscape?

grant funding and volunteer involvement to incorporate nice improvements throughout the length of the trail—the unique retaining wall on your left, a circular observation deck coming up on your right, and attractive ironwork bridges and railings throughout—which add aesthetic beauty and interest to the concrete jungle.

About 1 mile into your journey you'll come to a small wetlands area, restored from a gravel pit and dump site into a lush habitat for wildlife (and sometimes humans, too—an unfortunate reality of the urban hiking experience). Immerse yourself in this small yet mighty wetlands by following the path around a short loop—where you might spot an array of birdlife including herons, egrets, hawks, and more—before continuing on the main path, heading due east. As the path winds its way around several highway junctions, you'll pass another surprising wildlife encounter: a wide expanse of prairie dog colonies. Located right in the middle of the city, these critters don't need much vegetation to thrive, and greatly contribute to the surrounding ecosystem.

The trail turns into a mix of dirt and sand as you leave Commerce City and enter Denver proper, where it can become quite muddy during the winter and spring months (plans to pave this section are in the works). Here the trail gradually moves away from the freeway and into the residential area of Central Park (formerly known as Stapleton). Handsome suburban homes will come into view just before the junction that connects the Sand Creek trail to the neighborhood's own network of local parks and trails. Turning right here also leads to the Bluff Lake Nature Center and, eventually, Star K Ranch, both of which lie farther to the east.

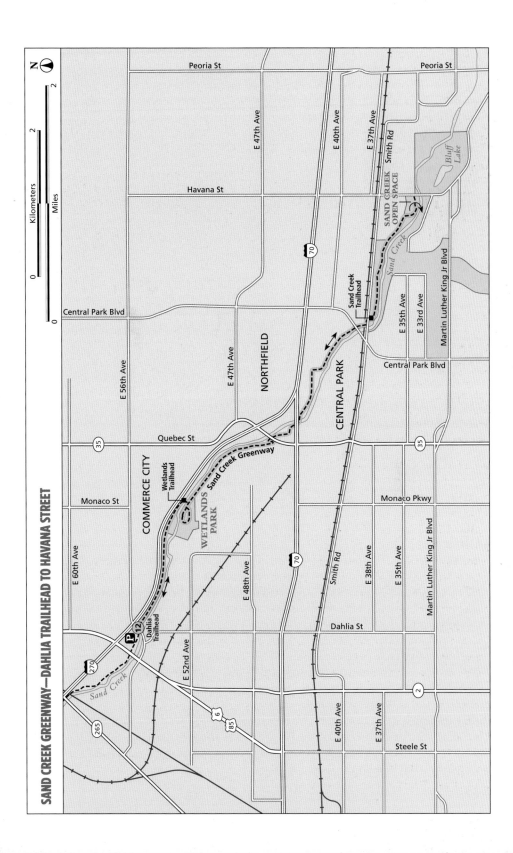

SAND CREEK GREENWAY—DAHLIA TRAILHEAD TO HAVANA STREET

Stay straight, continuing on the north side of the creek on your approach to the Sand Creek Open Space, a wide riparian area and prime habitat for migrating birds, coyotes, deer, rabbits, and more. As the trail moves toward the eastern plains in Aurora, the landscape gradually displays more low-moisture vegetation like rabbitbrush, cactus, and prairie grasses. Although the trail has been mostly flat so far, on the eastern end of this open space the terrain becomes more rocky, narrow, and steep. When you reach Havana Street, turn around and retrace your steps back to the trailhead. Or use a rideshare or shuttle service to catch a lift back to Dahlia Street.

MILES AND DIRECTIONS

0.0 Descend the staircase located on the southeast corner of the parking area, and begin walking southeast on the paved trail, with the creek on your right.

1.1 Turn right, then stay left to hike clockwise around the Wetlands Loop.

1.5 Continue straight to return to the main trail.

3.8 Stay right.

4.4 Continue straight, passing the Sand Creek Trailhead on your left.

5.0 When you reach Havana Street, turn around and retrace your steps back to the trailhead.

10.0 Arrive back at the trailhead.

LOCAL INTEREST

Four Friends Kitchen: Savor modern, scratch-made, Southern brunch specialties like shrimp and grits, chicken and waffles, and po'boy sandwiches on a shaded rooftop patio. 2893 Roslyn St., Denver; (303) 388-8299; fourfriendskitchen.com

Station 26 Brewing: Enjoy craft beer, food trucks, and live music in an indoor/outdoor setting, housed in a former fire station in the Park Hill neighborhood. 7045 E. 38th Ave., Denver; (303) 333-1825; station26brewing.co

LODGING

Best Western Plus Executive Residency: Simple, modern accommodations conveniently located in the Northfield shopping development, near the interstate, featuring an outdoor pool. 4590 Quebec St., Denver; (303) 320-0260; bestwestern.com/en_US/book/hotels-in-denver/best-western-plus-executive-residency-denver-central-park-hotel/propertyCode.06194.html

13 VAN BIBBER CREEK TRAIL

Located in a more rural part of the city, this open space area feels remote and restful—the perfect place for a trail run or walk—with meadow wildlife and mountain vistas.

Elevation gain: 146 feet
Distance: 4.8-mile loop
Hiking time: 1.5–2 hours
Difficulty: Easy to moderate, due to a hill on south side of park
Seasons: Year-round
Trail surface: Paved, dirt
Land status: Jefferson County Open Space Parks and Trails
Nearest town: Arvada
Other trail users: Cyclists, equestrians, E-bikes

Water availability: Yes, at Skyline Park
Canine compatibility: Yes, on leash
Fees and permits: None
Map: City of Arvada Parks & Open Space Trail Map & Guide: arvada.org/source/Sept2015%20Trail%20Map.pdf
Trail contact: Jefferson County Open Space: (303) 271-5925
Trailhead GPS: N39 47.87' / E105 09.89'

FINDING THE TRAILHEAD

 From downtown Denver, drive north on I-25 for about 2 miles to I-70 West. Drive west on I-70 for about 10 miles, then take exit 244 onto CO 72/Ward Road. Turn right on Ward Road and drive north. In about 1.5 miles, turn left on West 52nd Avenue, then right on Indiana Street. The trailhead parking area is on the right. (Van Bibber Park West/Indiana Trailhead: 5590 Indiana St., Arvada)

WHAT TO SEE

The Van Bibber Park and Open Space is a lovely, secluded area for hiking and horseback riding, with mesmerizing views of the foothills and a variety of amenities like picnic shelters, park benches, restroom facilities, and sports fields. Surrounded by residential neighborhoods and horse farms, the trail covers a few distinct landscapes, from a grassy meadow with wetland and riparian habitat, to an urban park setting with a playground and a pond. A lack of tree cover allows ample sunshine to keep the trail mostly free of snow, making this a great year-round hiking destination (on the flip side, a lack of shade makes this park very hot and dry in the summertime).

Start out hiking east from the Indiana (West) Trailhead on the paved path, which begins on the northeast corner of the parking area. On your right is a fenced-in wetlands conservation area full of cattails and shrubs, where an abundance of birds and other wildlife reside. Stay left, hugging the northern perimeter of the park, as you pass over rolling hills and through an expansive meadow. Although you can't always see it from the trail, stands of cottonwood trees indicate where the creekbed runs. As you approach Ward Road, serving as the eastern border of Van Bibber Park, several different trails will cross your path. Stay straight, continuing east toward the Ward Road Trailhead. At the trailhead, locate the trail on your left leading to an underpass, nicely developed with landscaping and a flagstone sign.

On the other side of the tunnel is a short neighborhood connector, popular with joggers, dog walkers, and cyclists. Soon you'll arrive at Skyline Park, a nice neighborhood park with a playground, tennis courts, restrooms, and water fountains. At the far end of

A dirt trail encircles this remote park offering a rugged feel and amazing scenery.

The trail ends at a small yet pretty lake where you can have a seat and witness an urban wetland environment.

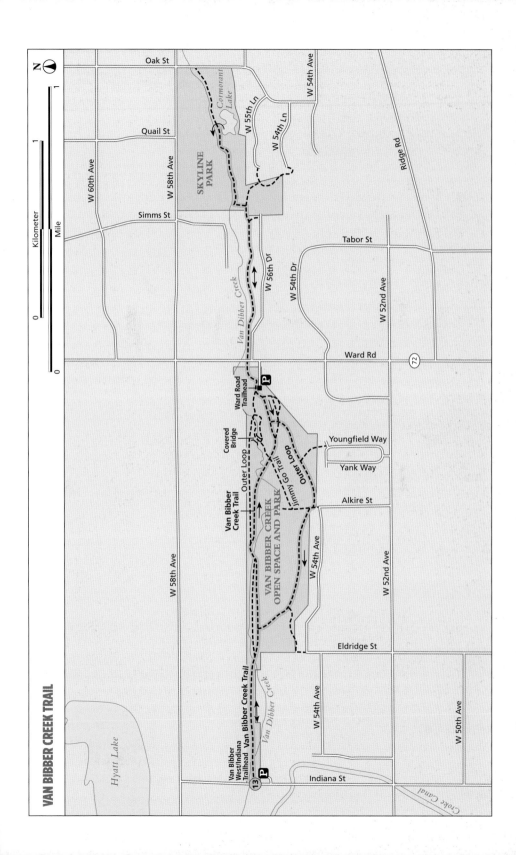

VAN BIBBER CREEK TRAIL

this park sits Cormorant Lake, surrounded by recreation facilities including the Apex Field House and the Stenger Sports Complex offering a multitude of outdoor sporting fields. Feel free to explore the short trail around the lake, where you might see ducks, geese, fish, and turtles. Afterward, return to the main trail and follow it back through Skyline Park to the Ward Road Trailhead.

Just past Ward Road, turn left off the paved path and onto a narrow dirt footpath. Here, instead of returning the same way you came, you'll head south to experience a different perspective of the surrounding area. The trail ascends a rocky hill and, when you stop to catch your breath at the top, you'll enjoy sweeping views of the foothills to the west and the valley below. As you wind your way down the other side of the hill, the trail surface changes from dirt to fine-crushed gravel, widening as it flattens out through the meadow. Continue following this path until it meets up with the paved trail. Turn left on the pavement, which will deliver you back to the trailhead shortly.

MILES AND DIRECTIONS

0.0 Begin walking east on the paved trail.

0.4 Stay straight on the paved path, or veer left for the dirt path.

0.5 Continue straight.

1.1 Continue straight, heading east toward the Ward Road Trailhead.

1.4 Arrive at the Ward Road Trailhead. Stay left toward the underpass at Ward Road/CO 72.

2.0 Turn left as you enter Skyline Park, continuing on the paved trail around the tennis courts, moving northeast.

2.3 Arrive at Cormorant Lake, your turnaround point. Walk the short loop around the lake, then retrace your steps back to the Ward Road Trailhead.

3.4 Stay left, turning onto a dirt trail leading south.

3.8 Follow the trail to the right, then stay left to continue on the dirt path, moving west.

4.1 Stay right.

4.3 Turn left, returning to the paved trail.

4.8 Arrive back at the parking area.

LOCAL INTEREST

New Terrain Brewing Company: Specializing in "exploratory" craft beers, this spacious taproom and beer garden is a great place to enjoy a post-hike refreshment. 16401 Table Mountain Pkwy., Golden; (720) 697-7848; newterrainbrewing.com

Edwards Meats: Grab a build-your-own deli sandwich from this butcher/market and plan a picnic in the park. Choose from a large assortment of high-quality deli meats, salads, and prepared sides. 12280 W. 44th Ave., Wheat Ridge; (303) 422-4397; edwards-meats.com

LODGING

Comfort Inn West Arvada Station: Basic yet comfortable accommodations conveniently located near I-70 and featuring an indoor pool. 10200 W. I-70 Frontage Rd. S., Wheat Ridge; (303) 422-6346; choicehotels.com/colorado/wheat-ridge/comfort-inn-hotels/co157?mc=llgoxxpx

14 RALSTON CREEK TRAIL— RALSTON CENTRAL PARK TO GOLD STRIKE PARK

This urban trail is a main recreational vein bisecting the city of Arvada, connecting neighborhoods, parks, and historic landmarks as it rolls alongside a pretty streamside corridor.

Elevation gain: 87 feet
Distance: 5.4 miles out and back
Hiking time: About 1.5 hours
Difficulty: Easy
Seasons: Year-round
Trail surface: Paved
Land status: City of Arvada
Nearest town: Arvada
Other trail users: Cyclists, equestrians
Water availability: Yes, at trailhead

Canine compatibility: Yes, on leash
Fees and permits: None
Map: City of Arvada Parks & Open Space Trail Map & Guide: arvada.org/source/Sept2015%20Trail%20Map.pdf
Trail contact: City of Arvada Parks, Golf & Hospitality Department: (720) 898-7400
Trailhead GPS: N39 48.14' / E105 05.86'

FINDING THE TRAILHEAD

From downtown Denver, take I-25 North to I-70 West. In about 5 miles, take exit 269A onto CO 121/Wadsworth Boulevard, then turn right. Turn left on Ralston Road in 1 mile, then right on Garrison Road in about 1 more mile. The parking area is on the right. (Ralston Central Park: 5850 Garrison St., Denver)

WHAT TO SEE

In 1850 Lewis Ralston extracted a gold nugget from the rocky creekbed along which this trail was formed, a discovery that helped kick off the great migration of the Pikes Peak Gold Rush. Ralston's namesake creek and trail is now the thread that connects a network of neighborhoods, parks, lakes, and landmarks throughout the city of Arvada, which manages some 3,400 acres of open space and 150 miles of trails. It is also recognized by the Arbor Day Foundation as a "Tree City USA" partner for its dedication to ensuring a healthy tree canopy that provides shade, beauty, and healthy wildlife ecosystems for the community.

The 12-mile Ralston Creek Trail is the longest trail in Arvada, stretching west to east from Blunn Reservoir to Gold Strike Park, but this hike covers a more manageable section through the town center on the eastern end. As always, you are more than welcome to continue exploring as far as your feet will carry you. You'll start in Ralston Central Park, offering nice amenities such as plenty of parking, a large picnic pavilion, restrooms, a memorial garden, two playgrounds, and a splash pad. The trail passes through many wonderful parks along the way, and also jogs through a few residential neighborhoods as necessary for continuity, so be sure to look for green trail signs if it gets confusing at any point.

Head northeast from the parking area on the paved trail. The park will quickly transition into yet another, called Hoskinson Park, a narrow strip of green space positioned

Cottonwood trees frame the foothills along the grassy bank of Ralston Creek, where one of the earliest gold discoveries in Colorado was made.

Even in the middle of winter, warm, sunny days are plentiful in the Mile High City.

parallel to Brooks Drive. At the corner of Ammons Street, follow the trail as it turns right, across a bridge and past a small playground, entering Memorial Park. Several city buildings can be found here, including City Hall and the police department, but the most interesting feature of this park is the Johnny Roberts Disc Golf course. This 18-"hole" course zigzags through the length of the park, attracting crowds year-round who aspire to toss weighted plastic discs into aboveground chain-link baskets. The rules are similar to golf, but the etiquette is much more casual and the atmosphere can get much more rambunctious. The sport has been gaining popularity in recent years and is popping up in urban areas more frequently, as it is an easy-access, low-cost outdoor activity. The game is entertaining to watch as you walk—just look out for erratic flying discs and be mindful of crowded pathways.

The trail exits the park on its northeast corner, where you are led on a short detour of sorts through a neighborhood street for a few blocks before rejoining the main trail at Wadsworth Boulevard. You are now in Creekside Park, another strip of land bordering a residential area, where the trail is popular with joggers and dog walkers. As you exit the park, moving into a more industrial area, be aware that this is where horseback riding is permitted to begin, so keep an eye out for (and be sure to yield to) equestrians. Next you'll arrive at Gold Strike Park (also known as the Lewis Ralston Gold Site), where antique mining machinery is on display in front of Spar Bridge, a 400-foot cable bridge, beyond which the creek merges with Clear Creek and continues eastward. Climb up on the bridge to check out the views, then turn around and return to the trailhead.

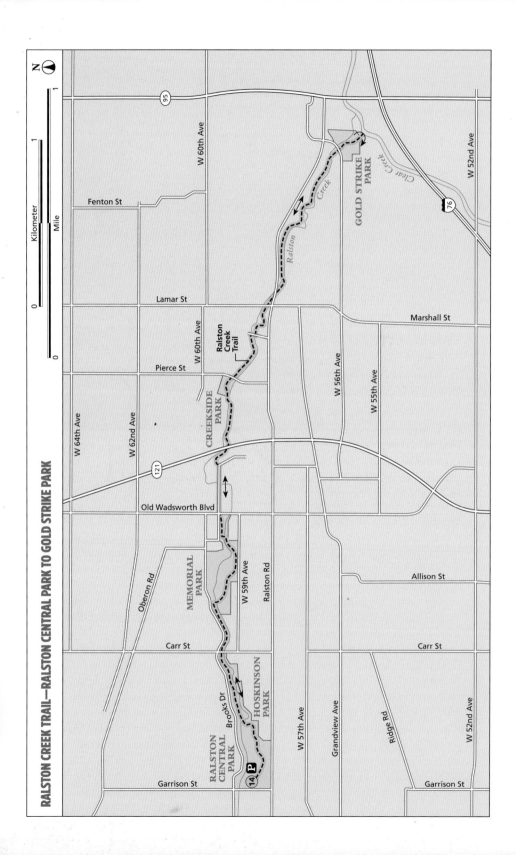

RALSTON CREEK TRAIL—RALSTON CENTRAL PARK TO GOLD STRIKE PARK

MILES AND DIRECTIONS

0.0 Locate the trail north of the parking lot and begin hiking east.

0.1 Stay right to continue east.

0.4 Continue straight, across the road.

0.6 Turn right to stay on the main trail, then continue straight.

0.72 Stay right to follow the main trail.

1.0 Travel east down West 60th Avenue.

1.2 Pick up the trail again at the intersection of 60th and Secrest Drive.

1.7 Safely cross Nolan Street as the trail jogs across the road to the right.

1.8 Stay left to continue on the main trail.

2.6 Cross the street toward the Gold Strike Park trailhead.

2.7 Cross the suspension bridge, then turn around and retrace your route back to the trailhead.

5.4 Arrive back at the Ralston Central Park trailhead.

LOCAL INTEREST

The Yak & Yeti Restaurant and Brewpub: A unique craft brewery with a full menu of Indian and Nepalese food, housed in a historic home in Olde Town Arvada. 7803 Ralston Rd., Arvada; (303) 431-9000; theyakandyeti.com/arvada

LODGING

Hilton Garden Inn Arvada Denver: Located just one-half block from the heart of Olde Town Arvada with modern accommodations featuring an indoor pool, on-site bar, and outdoor firepit. 5455 Olde Wadsworth Blvd., Arvada; (303) 420-9799; hilton.com/en/hotels/denavgi-hilton-garden-inn-arvada-denver

15 WEST LOOP TRAIL AT TWO PONDS NATIONAL WILDLIFE REFUGE

Although the trail system is quite small, this refuge is a treat for anyone seeking a quick and easy spot to walk, jog, and observe wildlife just steps from the city. As part of the national refuge system, it also offers an opportunity to learn more about the importance of wildlife protection, habitat conservation, and recreation access in urban areas.

Elevation gain: 38 feet
Distance: 0.8 mile lollipop loop
Hiking time: About 20 minutes
Difficulty: Easy
Seasons: Year-round
Trail surface: Dirt, gravel
Land status: US Fish & Wildlife Service
Nearest town: Arvada
Other trail users: None
Water availability: No

Canine compatibility: No dogs allowed
Fees and permits: None
Map: Two Ponds National Wildlife Refuge Trail Map: fws.gov/uploadedFiles/TwoPonds_MAP.pdf
Trail contact: Two Ponds National Wildlife Refuge: (303) 289-0232
Trailhead GPS: N39 50.40' / E105 06.52'

FINDING THE TRAILHEAD

From downtown Denver, take I-25 North for about 5 miles to US 36 West toward Boulder. In 2.5 miles, exit onto US 287 and keep right, then turn left on West 80th Avenue. Turn left into a medical center parking lot in 4.5 miles, just before the intersection of 80th Avenue and Kipling Street. Look for the trailhead sign on the south side of the parking lot (located on the northwest corner of the Two Ponds refuge area).

WHAT TO SEE

Spanning just 72 acres, the Two Ponds National Wildlife Refuge is the smallest preserve in the federal system, but nonetheless is teeming with wildlife and natural beauty. This urban refuge provides prairie, woodland, and wetland habitat for over 120 species of migrating birds and waterfowl, as well as several miles of natural-surface, hiker-only trails. Inconspicuously situated in between shopping centers and busy boulevards, the refuge also boasts a National Recreation Trail designation for providing an "urban population" with access to "high caliber" trails—one of just 1,300 trail systems in the country. The park is split into two territories: East and West. The main entrance is located on the east side, with trails encircling 9 acres of ponds and wetlands. Unfortunately, this area is only open from May through September. The west side, however, is open year-round and offers a more primitive trail system that meanders through rolling prairieland with panoramic views of the mountains.

To access the west-side trails, you'll park behind a medical center located on the corner of Kipling Street and West 80th Avenue. You'll see an informational signboard to

From the west side of the Two Ponds refuge, you can see spectacular views of snowcapped mountains in the foothills and beyond.

the south of this makeshift entrance, indicating the west-side trailhead. Stay left to begin hiking around the preserve clockwise. This first stretch of trail follows groves of willow and cottonwood trees around the north side of the park, parallel to a service road. You'll soon come to a set of bridges on your left, providing access to the east side of the refuge. If it is open (seasonally), you should cross over and explore the trail as far as you can, as it is quite scenic and serene, plus you can enter the "environmental education area" where the wetlands and ponds are located. If this area is closed, continue hiking south around the perimeter on the west-side trail. Here the landscape is a "prairie management area" where you might see coyotes, foxes, and deer roaming among sagebrush and yucca plants, or various birds of prey hunting for voles scurrying through the tall grasses.

At the southwest corner, follow the trail around a sharp corner to the right. You'll come to an intersecting trail on your right, which leads to a bench in the middle of the field you just walked around. The bench sits on a small hill and offers a nice 360-degree view of the surrounding meadow, providing a nice spot to sit for a while and absorb your surroundings (be forewarned that there is no shade here, however). Continuing north on the main path you'll soon come to yet another intersecting trail, this time coming in from the west (left) side. This path leads to a residential neighborhood with another makeshift entrance, with street parking, an information signboard, and trail markers. Just past this side path you'll move gradually uphill as you approach your starting point from the south. Here you're awarded with a magnificent view of some of the tallest mountains in the state.

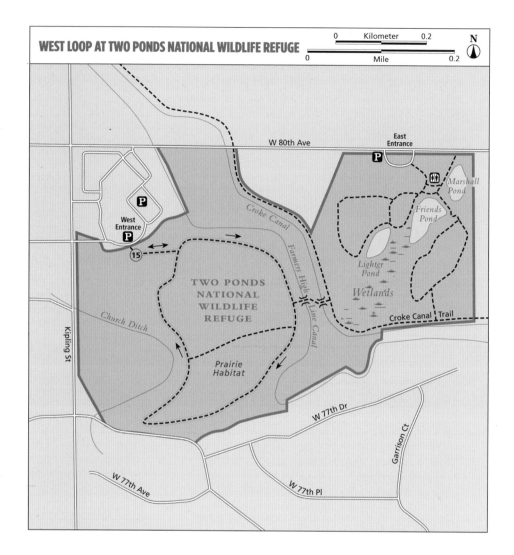

MILES AND DIRECTIONS

0.0 Locate the trail on the south side of the parking area and begin hiking east, staying left at the fork.

0.27 Continue straight.

0.5 Follow the path around a sharp corner to the right.

0.67 Stay right to continue on the loop.

0.8 Arrive back at the trailhead.

LOCAL INTEREST

The Butchery: This locally owned and operated white-tablecloth steakhouse located just around the corner from the east entrance of Two Ponds is popular for its "consistently craveable" menus for dinner, lunch, brunch, and everything in between. 7923 Allison Way, Arvada; (303) 425-1962; thebutcheryarvada.com

Sweet Bloom Coffee: Serious coffee drinkers won't want to skip a stop at this local roastery and cafe, which also offers classes on techniques like growing, grinding, and cupping for the home brewer. 7745 Wadsworth Blvd. #C, Arvada; (720) 360-9954; sweetbloomcoffee.com

Kokopelli Beer Company: This woman-owned and -operated brewery is heralded for its extensive menu, outdoor patio, and friendly neighborhood atmosphere. 8931 Harlan St., Westminster; (303) 284-0135; kokopellibeerco.com

LODGING

Hilton Garden Inn Arvada: Located within walking distance of the trendy historic district of Olde Town, this chain hotel features an outdoor firepit, indoor pool, and full bar on-site. 5455 Olde Wadsworth Blvd., Arvada; (303) 420-9799; hilton.com/en/hotels/denavgi-hilton-garden-inn-arvada-denver

16 LAKE MARY AND LAKE LADORA AT ROCKY MOUNTAIN ARSENAL NATIONAL WILDLIFE REFUGE

Featuring a variety of ecological habitats spread across some 15,000 acres of protected land, this sprawling wildlife enclave is a true urban respite just 8 miles from downtown Denver.

Elevation gain: 35 feet
Distance: 4.5-mile double loop
Hiking time: 1.5–2 hours
Difficulty: Easy
Seasons: Year-round
Trail surface: Dirt, boardwalk
Land status: National wildlife refuge
Nearest town: Commerce City
Other trail users: None
Water availability: Yes, at visitor's center

Canine compatibility: No dogs allowed
Fees and permits: None
Map: RMANWR Trail Map: fws .gov/uploadedFiles/RMANWR%20 Trail%20Map%2030x32%20georef .pdf
Trail contact: Rocky Mountain Arsenal National Wildlife Refuge: (303) 289-1930
Trailhead GPS: N39 48.87' / W104 52.80'

FINDING THE TRAILHEAD

From downtown Denver, take I-25 North to I-70 East. In about 4 miles, take exit 278 for Quebec Street, then turn left. Turn right on Prairie Parkway in about 2.5 miles, then left on Gateway Road. In 1 mile, turn left into the refuge entrance. Park at the Gateway Trailhead near the visitor's center. (6550 Gateway Rd., Commerce City)

WHAT TO SEE

The Rocky Mountain Arsenal National Wildlife Refuge is one of three such conservation areas in the Denver metro area and is a treasure trove of outdoor activities, including 20 miles of hiking trails, a wildlife driving tour, fishing lakes, and a nature center. Despite its wild allure, the terrain is tame, spanning everything from wetlands and woodlands to plains and prairie in just a few miles. The refuge was created, in part, to provide undisturbed habitat for bald eagles, and now this is one of the best places to catch a glimpse of these raptors in the region. The American bison is another iconic creature you can see here—the refuge introduced a herd in 2007 to graze on its sprawling grasslands (in other words, they help mow the lawn). This route will take you on a tour of Lake Mary and Lake Ladora on some of the property's most scenic, serene trails.

Be sure to stop in the visitor's center before starting your hike to get up-to-date information about recent wildlife sightings and trail closures. The facility also has a unique exhibit of black-footed ferrets as well as a kids' play area. From the center, walk east down the Discovery Trail toward the lakes. When you reach Lake Mary, turn left to begin the loop. The smaller of the two lakes harbors a wonderland of wildlife thanks to a tranquil wetlands and an island rookery. You will quickly come to a boardwalk that will transport you through a marsh full of cattails where birds, fish, and turtles like to take cover. Soon

The vivid colors of late summer blooming on the prairie.

after emerging from this immersive moment, turn left at the fork in the trail and ascend a small dam. From atop the dam road you can see an overview of Lake Ladora, a much larger water body ringed with gnarled cottonwood trees and small beaches. Use the "migration station" viewfinders to scan the area for wildlife activity before continuing on the main trail, which resumes east of the parking lot.

Now moving northeast, ahead of you lies vast prairieland as far as the eye can see. It is this expanse of property that the 11-mile self-guided wildlife drive encircles, where you can observe bison, antelope, deer, coyotes, foxes, and a slew of bird species in their natural habitat from a safe distance. The eastern edge of the lake is where you are most likely to find a moment of solitude, as many people don't venture much beyond Lake

This route makes a loop around not one, but two, beautiful lakes surrounded by native plants and animals.

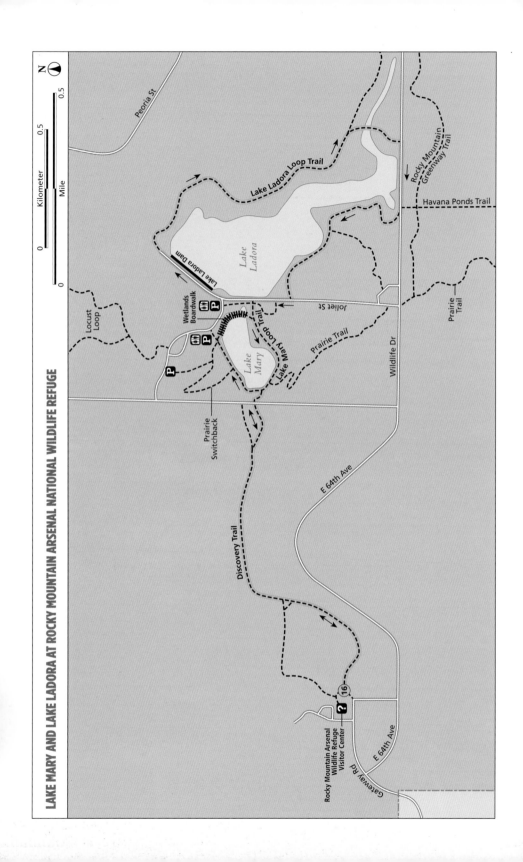

LAKE MARY AND LAKE LADORA AT ROCKY MOUNTAIN ARSENAL NATIONAL WILDLIFE REFUGE

Mary. Here there are park benches planted at the base of massive old trees, inviting you to sit awhile in the shade and gaze at the distant shadow of the foothills to the west. If you are patient you might see a cottontail darting beneath the rabbitbrush, or a heron fishing along the shore.

After crossing a bridge surrounded by cattails at the southeastern corner of the lake, you'll come to a road. Turn right and walk along the road for a short distance until you see the trail resume, heading north along the lake's western shore. Here the path dips even closer to the water's edge, with a few narrow stretches of sandy beach along the way where people come to fish and have picnics. Soon you'll find yourself back at the dam road. Turn right toward the dam, then descend the steps on the left toward Lake Mary. Turn left to walk along the south side of the smaller lake, where you'll get a good view of a small island rookery, as well as the distant city skyline with the mountains in the background. On the west side of the lake, turn left and return along the Discovery Trail to the visitor's center.

MILES AND DIRECTIONS

0.0 Locate the trail behind the visitor's center and begin hiking east, toward the lake.

1.0 Turn left to walk clockwise around Lake Mary.

1.2 At the Lake Mary Trailhead, stay right toward the wetlands boardwalk.

1.3 Turn left to ascend the dam, then left again to make your way around Ladora clockwise.

2.5 Turn right and walk along the road.

2.7 Turn right to rejoin the main trail, heading north.

3.2 Turn right and continue along the dam roadway.

3.3 Turn left to return to Lake Mary, then stay left to finish the loop.

3.6 Turn left to return to the visitor's center.

4.5 Arrive back at the trailhead.

LOCAL INTEREST

El Jardin: A popular Mexican restaurant that has been serving traditional dishes smothered with Southwestern green chile and fresh sopapillas on their breezy outdoor patio since the 1980s. 6460 E. 73rd Ave., Commerce City; (303) 288-3500; facebook.com/iLoveEljardin

LODGING

Best Western Premier Denver East: This modern, pet-friendly hotel features upscale amenities like poolside cabanas, EV charging stations, a full bar, and rooms with private patios. 4411 Peoria St., Denver; (303) 373-1444; bestwestern.com/en_US/book/hotels -in-denver/best-western-premier-denver-east/propertyCode.06195.html

17 WILDLIFE REFUGE TRAIL AT BARR LAKE STATE PARK

This Denver-area state park is one of the best birding spots around, and is particularly well-known for its healthy bald eagle population, which soars in early spring during nesting season. It features several well-maintained trails and a lovely nature center, too, making this a great day-trip destination.

Elevation gain: 10 feet
Distance: 5.7 miles out and back
Hiking time: 1–2 hours
Difficulty: Easy
Seasons: Year-round
Trail surface: Paved, dirt, boardwalk
Land status: Colorado State Parks
Nearest town: Brighton
Other trail users: Cyclists, equestrians
Water availability: Yes, at nature center
Canine compatibility: No dogs allowed in wildlife refuge; dogs allowed on leash in other areas of the park
Fees and permits: Fee required (pay at entrance)
Map: Barr Lake State Park Trail Use Map: cpw.state.co.us/placestogo/parks/barrlake/Documents/CPW_BAR_1of1.pdf
Trail contact: Colorado State Parks: (303) 659-6005
Trailhead GPS: N39 56.30' / E104 45.11'

FINDING THE TRAILHEAD

From downtown Denver, take I-25 North to exit 216A for I-76 East. In about 9.5 miles, take exit 22 onto Bromley Lane, then turn right. In about 1 mile, turn right onto Picadilly Road. In about 2 miles you'll see the entrance for Barr Lake State Park on the right. Stop at the entrance station to purchase or show your Parks Pass. Turn left at the fork toward the nature center and Prairie Welcome Trailhead (13401 Picadilly Rd., Brighton).

WHAT TO SEE

Located about 25 miles north of downtown Denver, Barr Lake State Park is an expansive area with several trails for hiking, biking, and horseback riding, as well as a 1,900-acre reservoir for fishing and boating (paddling and small motors only). But the biggest attraction the park has to offer is the protected wildlife refuge on the southwest end of the lake. An abundance of mature cottonwood trees around the lake have created a rookery for migratory birds and waterfowl, which is especially popular with a healthy bald eagle population that flocks to the park to nest and fish the serene waters, which are stocked with trout, catfish, bass, and walleye, to name a few (boats and fishing are not allowed on the south half of the lake, where the wildlife refuge is located).

Although the park offers a great place to hike year-round, it is an especially excellent spot to visit in the winter, during nesting season. During one visit on a particularly beautiful, sunny day in late February, I counted literally dozens of bald eagles before I even set foot on the trail, and at least a dozen more during my hike (not to mention several falcons and white pelicans, too). Although some trails may be closed seasonally to protect

An irrigation canal runs alongside the Perimeter Trail, adding serenity to the surroundings.

nesting areas, there are several designated observation sites along the way that offer great views of the rookery from a safe distance. Be sure to stop by the nature center before hitting the trail to learn about recent eagle activity and trail closures and to borrow a pair of binoculars for an even better view.

You'll start walking south on the Perimeter Trail, moving clockwise around the lake. After crossing the canal via a footbridge, turn left and look for signs pointing to the Neidrach Nature Trail on the right. This short, winding boardwalk provides interpretive signs with information about the surrounding prairie and wetland ecosystems that you will encounter on the rest of the hike. Turn left at the end of the path to continue on the main trail to the right. Here the trail curves around to the west, offering a nice view of the mountains across the plains. Although there are plenty of trees along the water's edge, be aware that the majority of the trail is fully exposed without much shade cover. You do get somewhat of a cooling, calming effect, however, as the trail is surrounded by water with the canal to the left and the lake to the right.

Next, you'll discover another "spur" trail called the Fox Meadow Loop featuring a boardwalk jutting over the marshy shoreline with an "observation station" where you can use a stationary viewfinder to look for signs of birds, fish, and other wetland wildlife activity. Soon after rejoining the main trail, you'll come to yet another spur leading to the Barr Lake Gazebo, offering a slightly different vantage point from which to study the lake in quiet solitude. If you don't see anything at either of these "wildlife watching" areas, close your eyes and listen instead for other signs of nature's bounty: the chatter of birds

The Rookery Gazebo is one of the best wildlife viewing spots around.

in the branches overhead, the rustle of squirrels scurrying around the forest floor, or the sound of the breeze blowing across the plains.

Next, the Perimeter Trail winds its way alongside a picturesque canal, where you may spot fish, fox, and birds bobbing around. You'll soon come to a final spur leading to the Inlet Gazebo—the most impressive of them all. This spur is not to be missed as it leads to a rookery viewing platform boasting a direct view of a multitude of eagle nests. While you may not be able to see into the nests with the naked eye, here you will most likely see adult raptors soar, fish, and preen themselves over the water right in front of you. Flocks of geese, pelicans, and a variety of duck species are commonly seen here, too. This spot is well-known by wildlife photographers as some 350 different species of birds and waterfowl have been spotted here over the years. The gazebo might be crowded with giant lenses on tripods, but don't be shy about bellying up to the railing to have a good look for yourself.

Once you've had your fill at the gazebo and find yourself back on the main trail, you can turn left and return to the trailhead to complete your trek, or turn right and continue exploring the Perimeter Trail, which continues around the lake for about 6 more miles in a complete loop that will eventually lead you back to the trailhead and nature center. On the far side of the lake you will find meadows full of prairie wildlife such as deer, foxes, and hawks; have a look at the dam, as well as a historic building that now houses the Bird Conservancy of the Rockies headquarters; and access a small fishing pier.

MILES AND DIRECTIONS

0.0 Cross the footbridge located on the west side of the Prairie Welcome Trailhead parking area.

0.4 Turn left to begin hiking south on the Perimeter Trail (paved).

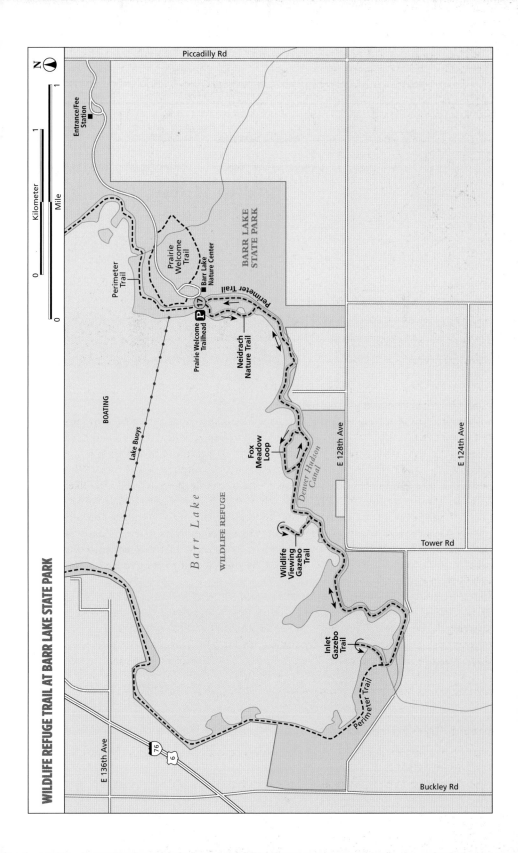

WILDLIFE REFUGE TRAIL AT BARR LAKE STATE PARK

N

Kilometer

Mile

Entrance/Fee Station

Piccadilly Rd

Perimeter Trail

Prairie Welcome Trail

Barr Lake Nature Center

BARR LAKE STATE PARK

Prairie Welcome Trailhead

P 17

Neidrach Nature Trail

Perimeter Trail

BOATING

Lake Buoys

Fox Meadow Loop

Denver Hudson Canal

Barr Lake

WILDLIFE REFUGE

Wildlife Viewing Gazebo Trail

E 128th Ave

E 124th Ave

Tower Rd

Inlet Gazebo Trail

Perimeter Trail

E 136th Ave

76
6

Buckley Rd

0.06 Stay right toward the Neidrach Nature Trail (dirt).

0.1 Stay right on the Neidrach Nature Trail.

0.35 Stay right.

0.37 Turn right to rejoin the paved Perimeter Trail.

1.0 Turn right on the Fox Meadow Loop trail to access the boardwalk viewing platform overlooking the lake.

1.3 Turn right to rejoin the paved Perimeter Trail.

1.6 Turn right to access the Barr Lake Gazebo via the out-and-back Boardwalk to Gazebo trail (or continue straight).

1.9 Turn right to continue on the paved Perimeter Trail.

3.0 Turn right to access the rookery viewpoint via the out-and-back Inlet Gazebo Trail boardwalk.

3.1 Arrive at the Rookery Gazebo wildlife viewing area. Retrace your steps back to the main trail.

3.3 Turn left to head back toward the main trailhead (or turn right to continue on the 8-mile Perimeter Trail).

4.3 At the junction, continue straight on the main trail.

4.6 At the junction, continue straight on the main trail.

4.8 Continue straight.

5.4 At the junction, turn left onto the dirt trail, then veer right, to complete the other half of the Neidrach Nature Trail loop.

5.6 Turn right, then left, to rejoin the main paved trail.

5.7 Turn right across the bridge to arrive back at the trailhead and nature center parking lot.

LOCAL INTEREST

Big Choice Brewing: Locally owned bar and restaurant serving fresh artisan pizzas and craft beers in a bright, airy taproom. Also offers deli sandwich meals for picnicking. 21 S. First Ave., Brighton; (303) 498-0150; bigchoicebrewing.com

La Estrellita Mexican Food: Family owned authentic Mexican restaurant with a colorful outdoor patio and creative selection of flavored margaritas. 45 N. Main St., Brighton; (303) 654-9900; laestrellitarestaurant.com

Berry Patch Farms: Family owned and operated pick-your-own farm operation featuring certified organic fruits and vegetables year-round, with seasonal events and children's programs. 13785 Potomac St., Brighton; (303) 659-5050; berrypatchfarms.com

LODGING

Holiday Inn Express & Suites Denver NE–Brighton: Modern and 100 percent smoke-free rooms with an indoor pool and hot tub on-site. Located adjacent to Barr Lake and near a major shopping center for convenience. 2212 Medical Center Dr., Brighton; (303) 659-8574; ihg.com/holidayinnexpress/hotels/us/en/brighton/denbt/hoteldetail

EAST METRO

It's a bird, it's a plane, it's . . . both! East Denver is rapidly flourishing into a metropolis all its own, thanks in part to its proximity to the ever-expanding Denver International Airport, one of the busiest airports in the country. Although you will see and hear planes overhead while hiking in this part of town, the quality of the scenery, trails, open spaces, and wildlife is not to be underestimated. Most of the hikes featured here are located within the sprawling city of Aurora, which manages some 8,000 acres of open space, 100 miles of trails, and three nature centers, two of which are featured in the following pages.

Plains and prairie habitats dominate the eastern landscape, which may come as a surprise to some who thought Denver was all rocks and aspen trees. Out here, deer and antelope literally roam among clumps of wispy blue grama (the Colorado state grass),

Commonly found along waterways, cottonwood trees are stunning year-round, from scraggly to lush to golden.

and the wind can blow tumbleweeds for miles along the flat, sparse terrain. The only real elevation you'll encounter out east is that of the towering cottonwood trees that line the creeks and lakes, offering a bit of much-needed protection from the intense Colorado sun. And although this is a relatively young residential and commercial area, the plains region has a long history of primitive homesteading, wagon trails, and hunting grounds, which you will learn about on each of these hikes.

Whether you're looking to shake off that stale airplane air during a long layover or are looking for a fresh spot to walk Spot near your new neighborhood or workplace, these hiking routes are convenient and educational, and offer scenic views as far as the eye can see.

18 HIGH LINE CANAL TRAIL— AURORA CITY CENTER TO STAR K RANCH

This portion of a popular regional commuter trail offers an introduction to one of the largest cities in the state, and a glimpse into city life on the eastern plains.

Elevation gain: 27 feet
Distance: 12.1 miles out and back
Hiking time: About 4 hours
Difficulty: Easy
Seasons: Year-round
Trail surface: Paved
Land status: City of Aurora
Nearest town: Aurora
Other trail users: Cyclists, joggers
Water availability: No
Canine compatibility: Yes, on leash
Fees and permits: None

Map: City of Aurora Trail Map: auroragov.org/UserFiles/Servers/ Server_1881137/File/Business%20 Services/Development%20 Center/Transit%20Oriented%20 Development/2nd/003235.pdf
Trail contact: City of Aurora Parks, Recreation & Open Space: (303) 739-7160
Trailhead GPS: N39 42.75' / E104 48.94'

FINDING THE TRAILHEAD

From downtown Denver, take I-25 North to I-70 West. In about 8 miles, take exit 282 on I-225 South. In 4 miles, take exit 8 onto Alameda Avenue, then turn left. In 0.5 mile, turn left into the Aurora Municipal Center parking lot. (Aurora Municipal Center: 14999 E. Alameda Ave., Aurora)

WHAT TO SEE

This section of the 71-mile High Line Canal Trail starts in the heart of Aurora and show-cases a few of the city's attractions, residential areas, and landscapes. You'll begin at City Center Park—located in a bustling commercial area in front of the Aurora Municipal Center, which houses the city's main public library, police department, history museum, and courthouse—and continue to Star K Ranch. Fully paved, this path has several road crossings as it navigates the urban landscape and offers a glimpse into the daily life of Colorado's third-largest city. To modify the route to make it shorter and easier, you can turn around at any point to return to the trailhead, or opt to use a transportation service, such as Lyft or Uber, to shuttle you back.

From the park, head toward the footbridge on the north side of the lake, which arches over the canal, then turn right to begin walking east on the trail. You'll soon come to Chambers Road, where a nice underpass has been constructed for a safe crossing. You'll emerge from the tunnel onto the city-owned DeLaney Farm Park and Historic District, home to a community garden as well as a collection of preserved structures. The white clapboard building on your left is the John Gulley Homestead House, the oldest home in town. Built in the late 1860s and added to the National Register of Historic Places in 1986, the structure is one of thirty-two landmarks included in the city's "Story Line"

The Aurora City Center Park anchors a variety of municipal offerings like a history museum, public library, and police department.

audio tour (visit auroragov.org/cms/One.aspx?portalId=16242704&pageId=16572394 for details).

Next the trail passes through an extensive colony of prairie dog dens. Watch your step, as they often dart across your path, chattering to each other and scurrying back and forth from one lumpy pile of dirt to the next. You'll cross another bridge and ascend to meet the road in order to navigate across West Toll Gate Creek, a beautiful, wide stream full of plants and birdlife. Here the trail intersects with another path, the Toll Gate Creek Trail, which juts off to the south. Stay straight on the canal trail as it jogs around this twisty intersection, and continue moving east. The trail meanders through a pretty riparian corridor, with willow and cottonwood trees offering plenty of bird chatter. You'll also have a panoramic view of the mountains to the west, including the snowcapped Mount Evans.

The path continues winding alongside the canal, passing by the Community College of Aurora, various residential neighborhoods, a high school football field, and an urban goat farm. When you get to Colfax Avenue, carefully cross the busy street on a slight diagonal via the stone boulevard. Soon after, you'll arrive at Norfolk Glen Park, a small neighborhood playground offering local access to the trail (and marking the completion of segment #22, a system adopted by the High Line Canal Conservancy that organizes the trail into twenty-seven bite-size portions).

After the park, you'll venture briefly into "section #23," where the landscape changes rapidly from urban to rural as the trail parallels the southern fenceline of Star K Ranch,

The High Line Canal Trail provides a scenic commuter connection for an array of residential neighborhoods.

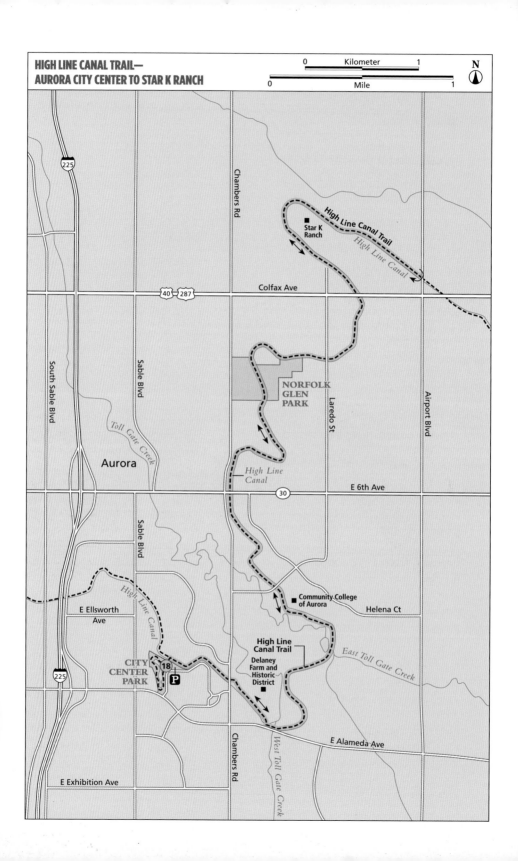

0   Kilometer   1

0   Mile   1

N

225

Star K Ranch

High Line Canal Trail

High Line Canal

Chambers Rd

Colfax Ave

40 287

Sable Blvd

South Sable Blvd

Toll Gate Creek

Aurora

NORFOLK GLEN PARK

Laredo St

Airport Blvd

High Line Canal

E 6th Ave

30

Sable Blvd

Community College of Aurora

Helena Ct

High Line Canal

E Ellsworth Ave

High Line Canal Trail

Delaney Farm and Historic District

East Toll Gate Creek

CITY CENTER PARK

18

P

225

West Toll Gate Creek

E Alameda Ave

E Exhibition Ave

Chambers Rd

lined with spiky yucca and sagebrush plants. You'll pass the junction for the Sand Creek Greenway, a 14-mile regional connector that cuts through the preserve, shortly before reaching your final destination of Airport Boulevard. You can retrace your steps back to the trailhead, or opt to take another form of transportation (such as a rideshare service like Uber or Lyft).

MILES AND DIRECTIONS

0.0   Locate the trail north of the Aurora Municipal Center parking lot.

0.05 Cross the footbridge, then turn right to begin hiking east.

0.38 Stay right toward the Chambers Road underpass/tunnel.

0.75 Follow the trail as it jogs over the bridge to the right and ascends to meet the road. Continue moving east-northeast and follow signs to stay on the main trail.

2.0   Continue straight, across East 1st Avenue.

2.6   Continue straight, across East 6th Avenue.

4.6   Continue straight, across East Colfax Avenue.

6.1   Arrive at Airport Boulevard. Turn around and retrace your steps back to the trailhead.

12.1 Arrive back at the City Center Park trailhead.

LOCAL INTEREST

Helga's German Restaurant & Deli: An authentic "Old World" family owned and operated establishment with a massive menu of schnitzels, wursts, pretzels, dumplings, and sandwich boards, plus ten genuine imported German beers on tap. 14197 E. Exposition Ave., Aurora; (303) 344-5488; helgasdeli.com

BJ's Brewhouse: A Colorado institution since 1878, this laid-back restaurant specializes in comfort food favorites—like ribs, pizza, and tacos—and has a full lineup of award-winning craft beers. Make sure to end your meal with their famous "pizookie," a chocolate-chip cookie baked (and served!) in a cast-iron skillet. 14442 E. Cedar Ave., Aurora; (303) 366-3550; bjsrestaurants.com

Parkside Eatery: The latest hipster food hall to hit the Denver dining scene is located in a brand-new, mixed-use development across the street from the Aurora Municipal Center and City Center Park, showcasing an array of restaurants and retailers surrounding a central bar area. 14531 E. Alameda Ave., Aurora; (303) 990-1441; parksideaurora.com

LODGING

Gaylord of the Rockies Resort & Convention Center: With eight restaurants and bars, an indoor/outdoor pool and water park, interactive virtual zoo safari, spa/salon services, and seasonal events and activities, this family-friendly behemoth has it all (and then some). 6700 N. Gaylord Rockies Blvd., Aurora; (720) 452-6900; marriott.com/hotels/hotel-information/details-13/dengr-gaylord-rockies-resort-and-convention-center

Best Western Plus Gateway Inn & Suites: Basic accommodations in proximity to a variety of amenities and conveniences, featuring an indoor pool. 800 S. Abilene St., Aurora; (720) 748-4800; bestwestern.com/en_US/book/hotels-in-aurora/best-western -plus-gateway-inn-suites

19 STAR K RANCH DOUBLE LOOP

Tucked down an unlikely alley in bustling Aurora, this diamond in the rough offers a peaceful place to escape from the demands of city life and quietly observe backyard wildlife in its natural habitat.

Elevation gain: 60 feet
Distance: 1.7-mile double loop
Hiking time: About 45 minutes
Difficulty: Easy
Seasons: Year-round
Trail surface: Dirt, sand, crushed gravel
Land status: City of Aurora
Nearest town: Aurora
Other trail users: Cyclists, equestrians

Water availability: Yes, at nature center
Canine compatibility: No dogs allowed in wetlands; dogs allowed on leash in other areas
Fees and permits: None
Map: Available at trailhead
Trail contact: City of Aurora Parks, Recreation & Open Space: (303) 739-7160
Trailhead GPS: N40 15.00'/ E 105 49.85'

FINDING THE TRAILHEAD

From downtown Denver, take I-70 East to exit 283. Turn right on Chambers Road, then left on East Smith Road, then right on Laredo Street. Look for signs for the Morrison Nature Center parking lot on your left. (16002 E. Smith Rd., Aurora)

WHAT TO SEE

Formerly the private property of Virgil "Pop" Stark, this serene site offers 250 acres of open space in the middle of the city of Aurora, the third-largest city in Colorado. Surrounded by warehouses and busy streets, the "ranch" showcases an array of ecosystems providing habitat for a multitude of wildlife, and 13 miles of natural-surface trails for walking, jogging, biking, and horseback riding. In addition to the preserve's own 0.5-mile Wetlands Loop and 1-mile Creekside Trail, two of the metro area's major regional connectors also pass through the property: the Sand Creek Greenway (14 miles total) and the High Line Canal Trail (71 miles total). This particular hike features a custom combination of several different trails for a nice "double-loop" tour.

Start out with a quick visit to the Morrison Nature Center, located on the east side of the parking lot, which was once the Stark family home and garage. Inside you'll find information about the park's wildlife and history, and meet a few reptilian friends in the process (make sure to grab a copy of the "Discover" brochure for a list of notable features that corresponds to numbered plaques displayed throughout the wetlands). Next, locate the Wetlands Loop Trail south of the nature center. Enter the trail to the left of the signboard, then stay right at the fork to move clockwise around the loop. This preserve is home to a number of animals, including turtles, raccoons, owls, and a variety of waterfowl. Surprisingly, it was also once home to alligators, parrots, and a chimpanzee—the curious collections of Mr. Stark's.

At the southwest corner of the wetlands habitat you'll come to a junction, anchored by a picnic pavilion. The wetlands loop continues to the right, but here you'll turn left, stepping onto the Sand Creek Greenway to explore the rest of the property. This portion of trail is often busy with people walking their dogs, jogging, and riding bikes and horses, but luckily it is plenty wide enough to accommodate everyone. After emerging from the towering trees that populate the wetlands, you are now out in the open with sweeping views (and no shade), heading southeast. Keep your eyes peeled for hawks, deer, and coyotes.

In about one-quarter mile, turn left to descend onto the Creekside Trail. As the name suggests, this dirt path rolls alongside Sand Creek through what is known as a "lowland riparian" habitat. Here the trail is lined with an abundance of vegetation, like cattails and cottonwood trees, creating a quiet, almost secretive, spot to stroll and look for critters in the creekbed. The trail will dead-end on the Sand Creek Greenway, where you will turn right to return to the picnic pavilion. Turn left at the pavilion to complete the Wetlands Loop Trail, which will return you to the nature center.

Even in winter, the wetlands area at the Morrison Nature Center is quietly teeming with wildlife.

A band of iron horses runs off into the sunset near the Morrison Nature Center on a late winter afternoon.

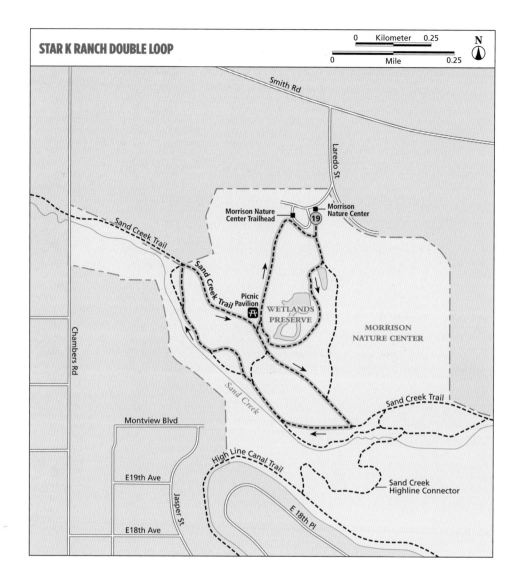

STAR K RANCH DOUBLE LOOP

MILES AND DIRECTIONS

0.0 Begin walking south from the nature center toward the information sign.

0.02 Stay left at the signboard to enter the wetlands.

0.08 Stay right on the Wetlands Loop trail.

0.38 Turn left at the picnic pavilion.

0.4 Turn left onto the Sand Creek Greenway trail.

0.45 Continue straight on the Sand Creek Greenway.

0.58 Continue straight.

0.66 Turn right down a dirt path to the Creekside Trail.

0.9	Stay left/continue straight.
1.2	Turn right onto the Sand Creek Greenway.
1.4	Turn left, moving toward the picnic pavilion, then continue straight.
1.6	Turn right to complete the final portion of the wetlands loop.
1.7	Arrive back at the nature center.

LOCAL INTEREST

Cora Faye's Cafe: An authentic soul food kitchen full of character serving "century-old family recipes," from classics such as fried chicken, collard greens, and mac and cheese to obscure Southern dishes like oxtail, frog legs, and pig's feet. 16251 E. Colfax Ave., Denver; (303) 333-5551; corafayescafe.com

Dry Dock Brewing—North Dock: This production facility for one of Colorado's top breweries offers a twelve-tap tasting room, pizza menu, home brewing classes, and an 18-hole disc golf course. 2801 Tower Rd., Aurora; (303) 400-5606; drydockbrewing.com/locations-hours/north-dock

LODGING

Denver Airport Marriott Gateway Park: An exceptional property with a lovely pool, hot tub, and fitness center as well as an on-site restaurant and market. 16455 E. 40th Circle, Aurora; (303) 371-4333; marriott.com/hotels/travel/dengp-denver-airport-marriott-at-gateway-park

20 TOLL GATE CREEK TRAIL—HORSESHOE PARK TO QUINCY RESERVOIR

This urban greenway closely follows a creek corridor with multiple neighborhood access points, providing a pleasant retreat into nature for a few moments of peace and quiet in the busy city of Aurora.

Elevation gain: 157 feet
Distance: 8.5 miles out and back
Hiking time: 2.5-3 hours
Difficulty: Easy
Seasons: Year-round
Trail surface: Paved
Land status: City of Aurora
Nearest town: Aurora
Other trail users: Cyclists
Water availability: No
Canine compatibility: Yes, on leash
Fees and permits: None

Map: City of Aurora Parks, Recreation & Open Space Toll Gate Creek Trail Map: auroragov.org/ UserFiles/Servers/Server_1881137/ File/Departments/PROS/Trail%20 Maps/TollgateCreekTrail_8.5x11.pdf
Trail contact: City of Aurora Parks, Recreation & Open Space: (303) 739-7160
Trailhead GPS: N39 40.72' / E104 47.97'

FINDING THE TRAILHEAD

From downtown Denver, take I-25 South for about 10 miles to I-225 North. In about 5.5 miles, take exit 5 onto Iliff Avenue, then turn right. In about 1 mile, turn left on Kittredge Way, then left into the parking lot. (Horseshoe Park: 2125 S. Kittredge Way, Aurora)

WHAT TO SEE

The Toll Gate Creek Trail provides access to a natural stream, open space, and a variety of recreational opportunities for the residents and neighbors of thousands of homes along its path, which provide a buffer from road noise. At any given time you might find people here riding bikes, walking their dog, feeding the ducks, bird-watching, or just lounging on a park bench. Although the trail technically begins about 2 miles farther north near the Delaney Farm Park, with many neighborhood access points throughout, the Horseshoe Natural Area makes a nice starting point thanks to ample parking and restroom facilities. Several regional trails converge in this 110-acre park, which also features a wetlands area and baseball fields, offering several options to explore the area further if you wish.

Start by walking northeast from the parking area, and look for a bridge on your right, north of the baseball fields. After crossing the bridge, turn right and look for signs directing you toward the main trail, moving south along Toll Gate Creek. You'll be right next to the creek—which often resembles a canal, with deep sides carved in concrete—for the duration of the hike, where rows of willow trees grow along the banks, sheltering birds, turtles, and waterfowl. Cottonwood and pine trees also dot the greenway flanking the creek, offering shade, although the trail is fully exposed for the most part, which creates a clear trail year-round thanks to the sunshine it receives.

Heading north, the wide-open expanse of the Toll Gate Creek Greenway offers unobstructed views of Longs Peak in the distance.

The trail winds through the Toll Gate Creek Greenway, a lush riparian corridor full of native plant and bird species.

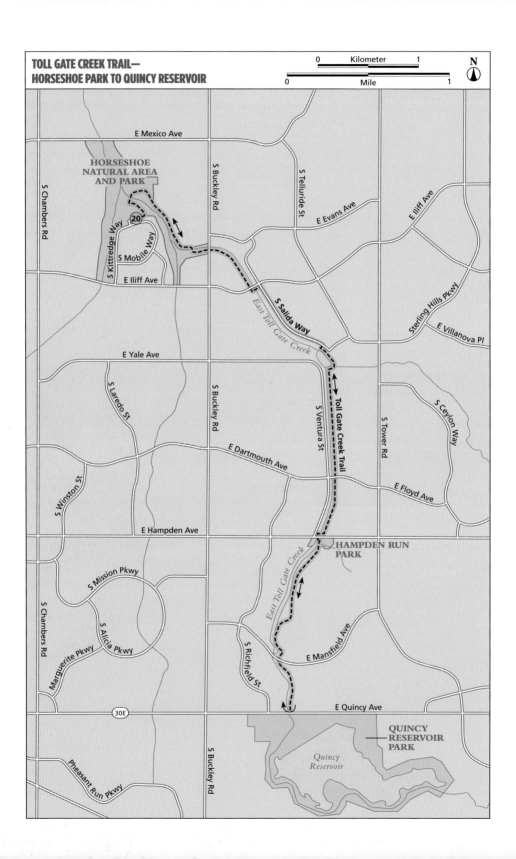

0   Kilometer   1

0   Mile   1

N

E Mexico Ave

HORSESHOE
NATURAL AREA
AND PARK

S Chambers Rd

S Buckley Rd

S Telluride St

E Evans Ave

E Iliff Ave

S Kittredge Way

20

S Mobile Way

E Iliff Ave

East Toll Gate Creek

S Salida Way

Sterling Hills Pkwy

E Villanova Pl

E Yale Ave

S Laredo St

S Buckley Rd

S Ventura St

Toll Gate Creek Trail

S Tower Rd

S Ceylon Way

E Dartmouth Ave

E Floyd Ave

S Winston St

E Hampden Ave

HAMPDEN RUN
PARK

S Mission Pkwy

S Alicia Pkwy

East Toll Gate Creek

E Mansfield Ave

S Chambers Rd

Marguerite Pkwy

30E

S Richfield St

E Quincy Ave

QUINCY
RESERVOIR
PARK

Quincy
Reservoir

Pheasant Run Pkwy

S Buckley Rd

After about 2 miles of winding along through residential areas, you'll come to a small pond offering a nice, protected area for waterfowl to gather, including seagulls, pelicans, ducks, and Canada geese. From the south side of this water feature, you can get a glimpse of the mountains to the north, including 14,259-foot Longs Peak, the highest peak in Rocky Mountain National Park.

Continuing south, you'll cross over and under a few roads before turning right at an ironwork bridge, signaling the entrance into Hampden Run Park, a lush, tranquil (unofficial) nature preserve. Although still closely overlooked by dense neighborhoods, the area is full of trees and teeming with wildlife. Watch for deer, coyotes, rabbits, and birds, including birds of prey hunting overhead. Soon the trail will come to an end at Quincy Avenue, with the dam forming Quincy Reservoir rising in front of you. Here you will turn around and retrace your path back to the trailhead at Horseshoe Park.

MILES AND DIRECTIONS

0.0 From the parking lot, walk northeast on the trail, moving counterclockwise around the ball fields.

0.19 On the northeast corner of the fields, turn right and cross the creek via the foot-bridge, then turn right.

0.26 Turn right.

0.33 Turn right.

0.78 Cross the bridge on the right.

0.81 Turn left to continue on the trail.

0.88 Stay left.

1.3 Cross Iliff Avenue and follow the trail to the left, then the right.

3.0 Follow the trail as it winds up and over East Hampden Avenue.

4.3 Turn around at East Quincy Avenue and retrace your steps back to the trailhead.

8.5 Arrive back at Horseshoe Park.

LOCAL INTEREST

Athenian Restaurant: A cozy, authentic Greek restaurant with creative decor and a menu to match, including a selection of "Dinner For Two" dishes for a romantic evening. 15350 E. Iliff Ave., Aurora; (720) 449-0224; theathenianrestaurant.com

Pearl of Siam: This female owned and operated Thai restaurant earns rave reviews for its fresh, authentic flavors—most of which are notoriously spicy. 18660 E. Hampden Ave., Aurora; (303) 617-7408; pearlofsiam.net/pearl/welcome

LODGING

DoubleTree by Hilton Denver–Aurora: Modern accommodations featuring soothing, natural color palettes, an indoor pool, complimentary airport shuttle, and on-site Jackdaw restaurant and bar. 13696 E. Iliff Pl., Aurora; (303) 337-2800; hilton.com/en/hotels/denitdt-doubletree-denver-aurora

21 SODDIE LOOP AT THE PLAINS CONSERVATION CENTER

This short loop will give you a taste of what life was like for early settlers on the prairie—a unique and harsh environment that required creativity and adaptation in order to survive—and a chance to view pronghorn antelope in the wild.

Elevation gain: 46 feet
Distance: 1.0-mile loop
Hiking time: About 30 minutes
Difficulty: Easy
Seasons: Year-round
Trail surface: Dirt
Land status: City of Aurora
Nearest town: Aurora
Other trail users: None

Water availability: Yes, at nature center
Canine compatibility: No dogs allowed
Fees and permits: None
Map: Available at the trailhead
Trail contact: Plains Conservation Center: (303) 326-8380
Trailhead GPS: N39 39.38' / E104 44.21'

FINDING THE TRAILHEAD

From downtown Denver, take I-25 South for 6 miles to I-225 North. In 4 miles, take exit 4 onto Parker Road/CO 83, then stay right. After about 1 mile on Parker Road, turn left on Hampden Avenue. Turn right into the entrance at Picadilly Road in about 5 miles. (Plains Conservation Center: 21901 E. Hampden Ave., Aurora)

WHAT TO SEE

The Plains Conservation Center offers a unique opportunity to learn about eastern Colorado's prairie ecosystem and the daily life of early settlers who homesteaded in the area in the mid-1800s. The 1,100-acre preserve has almost 7 miles of soft-surface trails that roll along across an expansive grassland and through a riparian corridor (closed seasonally for raptor nesting). Despite the seemingly harsh, barren landscape, the area is teeming with wildlife that thrives in this environment, including herds of pronghorn antelope that roam the hills, rattlesnakes lurking under clumps of sagebrush, and bald eagles that fish in East Toll Gate Creek, which bisects the property north to south.

At just 1 mile long, the Soddie Loop Trail is perfect for families with children, who will be delighted to explore the collection of historic structures, which include a blacksmith shop and schoolhouse, as well as a traditional tipi camp. Begin your hike at the visitor's center to pick up a trail map and learn a bit about the wildlife, history, and purpose of the preserve. Be sure to also grab the self-guided tour brochure, which corresponds to numbered markers along the trail offering factoids about various points of interest.

To begin your hike, cross the parking lot to the east and walk down the wide, dirt path called the North Soddie Loop trail, lined with pieces of antique farming equipment. Right away you'll notice the vastness of the area, a signature trait of the plains habitat: Low moisture means low vegetation, which means no shade from tree cover and no protection from wind (even though this is a short trail, be sure to apply sunscreen, and

Keep your eyes and ears open for resident critters that thrive in the prairie environment, like this well-camouflaged cottontail rabbit.

take sunglasses and water with you). On the plus side, there is nothing obstructing the view for miles. To the north you can see the unusual, white, balloon-like structures called "radomes," which are used to house satellites and other surveillance equipment at the Buckley Air Force Base, with the foothills stretched out behind them.

You'll quickly come to the replica tipi village on your right (this is stop #1 on your self-guided tour brochure). Next, on your left, is another trail, which leads to the stream. Feel free to take a quick jaunt down this short spur, returning to your starting point on the main loop afterward. Continuing east on the North Soddie Loop, you'll soon arrive at the Sod Village. This replica of a homestead built in the 1880s features several structures built with stacks of prairie sod instead of wood, due to the lack of trees in the area. In addition to houses and outbuildings, there is a chicken coop and corral that house live animals during the summer months for visitors to interact with. Be sure to keep your eyes peeled for signs of wild animals, too, like prairie dogs, rabbits, and snakes. There is also a picnic shelter here, which makes a nice place to rest in the shade.

After the Sod Village, the trail rounds a corner and heads west on the South Soddie Loop trail. This side of the route is more remote, with no structures save for a few prairie dog dens and an abundance of yucca and cactus plants. To complete the loop, you'll turn right as the trail meets up with the entrance road, which will return you to the nature center.

The Plains Conservation Center offers hiking trails, educational exhibits, wildlife encounters, and views as far as the eye can see.

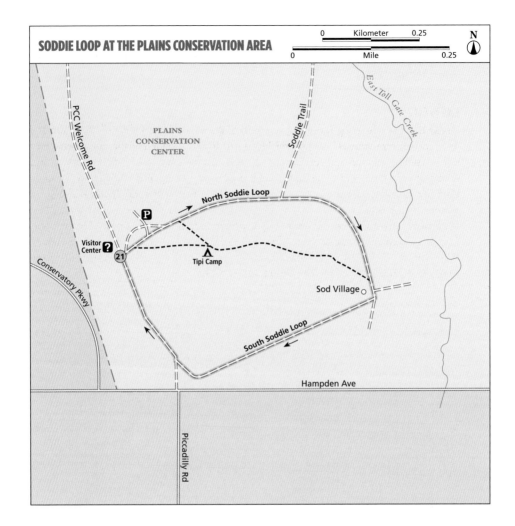

MILES AND DIRECTIONS

0.0 Locate the trail across the parking lot, east of the nature center.

0.5 Arrive at the Sod Village on the eastern end of the loop.

0.75 Turn right to walk down the paved driveway to the nature center.

1.0 Arrive back at the nature center.

LOCAL INTEREST

K+ Hot Pot: A unique Asian bistro with a self-serve conveyor belt whipping out steaming bowls of flavorful broth, noodles, and seafood boils, and exotic offerings like fish balls and lychee lemonade. 21699 E. Quincy Ave., Aurora; (303) 690-4066; kplushotpot.com

Two22 Brew: This community-conscious watering hole has a full calendar of social events from fitness clubs to food trucks, and donates a portion of every purchase to help local charities. 4550 S. Reservoir Rd., Centennial; (720) 328-9038; two22brew .com/#home1-section

LODGING

Great Escape Mustang Sanctuary & Eco Cabins: Intrigued by life on the plains and want to immerse yourself even more? Head east to this unique collaboration between a horse rescue operation and the Bureau of Land Management, where you can sleep in a solar-powered cabin and wake up to watch wild mustangs grazing outside your window. Daytime tours are also available. 42132 Ridge Rd., Deer Trail; (303) 621-7752; great escapesanctuary.org

Radisson Hotel Denver–Aurora: Sophisticated accommodations near Cherry Creek State Park with an on-site restaurant/bar and Enterprise car rental center. 3155 S.Vaughn Way, Aurora; (720) 678-9956; radissonhotels.com/en-us/hotels/radisson-aurora?cid=a:s e+b:gmb+c:amer+i:local+e:rad+d:us+h:USADSCO

The mountains actually are as close as they appear in the South Denver area, which is situated very near the base of the western foothills.

SOUTH METRO

Comprising sprawling suburban cities like Littleton, Centennial, Englewood, and Greenwood Village, southern Denver is largely residential. In addition to larger commercial and retail zones like the Denver Tech Center and the Park Meadows Mall, many of these towns feature their own quaint "main street" district lined with boutiques, coffee shops, and cultural offerings like museums, theaters, and libraries. Historic downtown Littleton is an especially charming area, with direct access to the South Platte River and Mary Carter Greenway Trails.

Due to the curve of the foothills and the lack of tall buildings, the mountains appear closer here and the sky seems more vast, which makes for excellent hiking scenery. The South Platte River and High Line Canal are the two main waterways around which many miles of recreational paths have been created, but there are also a plethora of parks, open spaces, nature centers, and gardens that prove to be nice places to stroll, too.

The South Denver region is spacious, scenic, serene, and perfect for strolling.

22 HIGH LINE CANAL TRAIL— EAST ORCHARD ROAD TO THREE POND PARK

This bucolic section of the 71-mile High Line Canal Trail is surrounded by old cottonwood trees, a nature preserve, and some of the most exclusive residential properties in the region.

Elevation gain: 28 feet
Distance: 11.4 miles out and back
Hiking time: About 4 hours
Difficulty: Easy
Seasons: Year-round
Trail surface: Dirt
Land status: City of Greenwood Village, Arapahoe County Open Space, city of Cherry Hills Village
Nearest town: Greenwood Village

Other trail users: Equestrians, joggers, cyclists
Water availability: Yes, at trailhead
Canine compatibility: Yes, on leash
Fees and permits: None
Map: High Line Canal Conservancy Digital Maps: highlinecanal.org/guide
Trail contact: High Line Canal Conservancy: (720) 767-2452
Trailhead GPS: N39 36.58' / E104 56.44'

FINDING THE TRAILHEAD

From downtown Denver, drive south on I-25 for about 11 miles to exit 198 for Orchard Road. Turn right on Orchard Road, then right into the trailhead parking lot in about 2.5 miles.

WHAT TO SEE

Starting in Waterton Canyon, about 20 miles south of downtown Denver, and stretching north to Green Valley Ranch, about 20 miles northeast of Denver (near the airport), the 71-mile High Line Canal Trail provides access to outdoor recreation and nature for some 350,000 Denver-area residents who live within 1 mile of its path. Owned and operated by Denver Water, the canal was built in 1883 to transport water from the South Platte River for irrigation purposes, with water flowing from April through October. The High Line Canal Conservancy—a nonprofit organization formed to promote stewardship and education of this National Landmark Trail, whose headquarters is located adjacent to the trailhead—created a system to split the trail into twenty-seven segments for greater manageability. It has also identified five distinct "character zones" to categorize each segment by the type of landscape each exhibits, showcasing a diverse array of ecosystems across the metro area.

This hike covers Segments 12 and 13, passing through the affluent suburban cities of Greenwood Village and Cherry Hills Village. Noted as a "Wooded Village" zone, this 6-mile section will impart a deep sense of tranquility from the get-go as it winds along the canal in the shade of massive, old-growth cottonwood trees, passing jaw-dropping homes and rolling acres of horse farms, with panoramic mountain views. The wide, flat path provides plenty of room for dog walkers, strollers, cyclists, and horses, as this is a very popular local route (proper trail etiquette suggests bikes yield to pedestrians, and

A wide, soft-surface path offers space for an array of recreational uses.

all users yield to equestrians). Numerous meadows and parks flank this section, offering a serene, rural atmosphere with plenty of wildlife viewing opportunities—especially for bird watchers.

One of these areas is the Marjorie Perry Nature Preserve, named for an adventurous outdoorswoman who owned a ranch on this land in the 1930s. The canal makes a sweeping switchback through the preserve, creating a picturesque spot for listening to birds chattering in the trees, watching for deer and coyotes roaming through a field of tall grasses and wildflowers, and gazing at the snowcapped mountains to the west, including Mount Evans standing tall at 14,265 feet in elevation, one of the most famous of the Front Range "fourteeners."

After the preserve you'll pass through a tunnel underneath Belleview Avenue, marking the border between Greenwood Village and Cherry Hills Village, and the beginning of Segment 13. Continuing north you'll enjoy more of the same tree-lined dirt path, with massive homes presiding over the canal on your right, and mountain views on your left. You'll notice several handsome footbridges arching over the stream along the way, offering private trail access to neighborhoods and farms—a trail rider's dream. One of these bridges also leads to the Dahlia Trailhead, a small park offering public trail access. Across from this is Blackmer Common, an open space with a small lake, former property of the sprawling, exclusive Kent Country Day School next door.

Categorized as a "Wooded Village" section, the
trail is surrounded by public open space and
private farmland creating a rural atmosphere.

This section of the 71-mile High Line Canal Trail marks the historic route's halfway point.

You'll pass a pretty wildlife preserve and pond just before crossing Quincy Avenue, which is about the halfway point of the full trail (wooden mile marker posts are installed along the route—look for mile marker 35 on the west side of the path). Continue on until you reach Three Pond Park, marking the end of Segment 13 and your final destination for this hike. The trail continues on for miles, of course, and you are welcome to continue exploring. Otherwise, turn around and retrace your steps back to the East Orchard Road Trailhead (or call a rideshare service, such as Uber or Lyft, to assist).

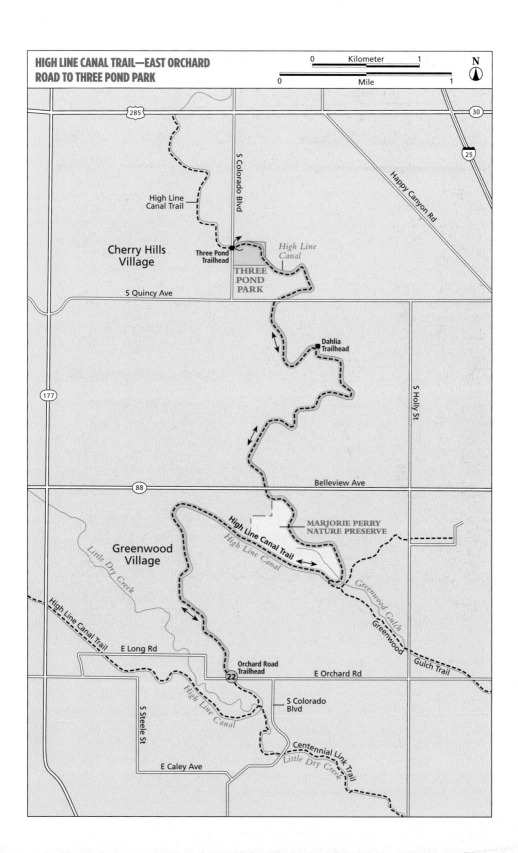

0   Kilometer   1

0   Mile   1

N

285

30

25

Happy Canyon Rd

High Line Canal Trail

S Colorado Blvd

High Line Canal

Cherry Hills Village

Three Pond Trailhead

THREE POND PARK

S Quincy Ave

Dahlia Trailhead

177

S Holly St

88

Belleview Ave

High Line Canal Trail

High Line Canal

MARJORIE PERRY NATURE PRESERVE

Greenwood Village

Little Dry Creek

High Line Canal Trail

Greenwood Gulch

Greenwood Gulch Trail

E Long Rd

Orchard Road Trailhead

22

E Orchard Rd

High Line Canal

S Steele St

S Colorado Blvd

Centennial Link Trail

E Caley Ave

Little Dry Creek

MILES AND DIRECTIONS

0.0 Locate the trail on the southwest corner of the parking area. Turn right to begin hiking north. This is the start of Segment 12.

2.9 Cross Belleview Avenue. This is the start of Segment 13.

5.7 Arrive at the Three Pond Trailhead. This is the end of Segment 13. Turn around and retrace your steps back to the Orchard Road Trailhead.

11.4 Arrive back at the Orchard Road Trailhead.

LOCAL INTEREST

Los Chingones: An energetic, Baja-style Mexican kitchen from a reputable Denver-based restaurateur with happy hour specials and an outdoor patio. 4959 S. Newport St., Denver; (303) 567-4258; loschingonesmexican.getbento.com/location/dtc/

Cherry Hills Sushi Co.: A modern yet inviting neighborhood sushi bar with an extensive selection of Japanese whiskey and sake. 1400 E. Hampden Ave., Cherry Hills; (303) 761-1559; cosushico.com

Barnhouse Tap: A brewery that gives a nod to the neighborhood's horse farm heritage, featuring a full bar (including forty-plus Colorado craft beers), a pizza menu, and an outdoor area with live music and lawn games. 4361 S. Broadway, Englewood; (720) 523-0201; barnhousetap.com

Fiddler's Green Amphitheatre: Catch a show at this intimate concert venue on a grassy lawn under the lights of the Denver Tech Center. 6350 Greenwood Plaza Blvd., Greenwood Village; (303) 220-7000; fiddlersgreenamp.com

LODGING

Hyatt Regency Tech Center: Located just 3 miles from the trailhead, this upscale property offers an indoor pool, complimentary shuttle service, and proximity to The Landmark, a shopping, dining, and entertainment hub. 7800 E. Tufts Ave., Denver; (303) 779-1234; hyatt.com/en-US/hotel/colorado/hyatt-regency-denver-tech-center/denver

23 MARY CARTER GREENWAY IN SOUTH PLATTE PARK

Running the length of the South Platte Park open space—an urban oasis with a smattering of lakes, trees, and trails—this trail offers a pleasant place to stroll just minutes from downtown Littleton, where you can eat, drink, and shop the rest of the day away.

Elevation gain: 48 feet
Distance: 5.0-mile figure-eight loop
Hiking time: 1–2 hours
Difficulty: Easy
Seasons: Year-round
Trail surface: Paved
Land status: City of Littleton
Nearest town: Littleton
Other trail users: Cyclists
Water availability: Yes, at nature center

Canine compatibility: Yes, on leash
Fees and permits: None
Map: South Suburban Parks & Recreation District Map: ssprd.org/Portals/0/Parks/DistrictMap.pdf
Trail contact: South Suburban Parks and Recreation: (303) 798-5131
Trailhead GPS: N39 35.02' / W105 01.72'

FINDING THE TRAILHEAD

From downtown Denver, drive south on Broadway for about 3.5 miles, then turn right on Iowa Avenue. Turn left on US 85/Santa Fe Drive and drive south for about 8 miles. Turn right on West Mineral Avenue, then right on South Platte River Parkway, then left on West Carson Drive. The road will dead-end at the Carson Nature Center parking lot. (South Platte Park Trailhead at Carson Nature Center: 3000 W. Carson Dr., Littleton)

WHAT TO SEE

The Mary Carter Greenway is an extension of the 32-mile South Platte River regional trail into the quaint community of Littleton, starting near the city's northern border around Union Street and culminating at the South Platte Reservoir. This 11-mile "addition" continues alongside the slow-moving South Platte River, traveling through Littleton's historic downtown district and past several local points of interest, and through a series of small lakes with several superb spots for watching wildlife, taking photos, and simply enjoying the scenery (the mountains seem magnified here, as Littleton sits slightly farther west than Denver). This hike focuses on the southernmost 2.5 miles of trail located within the 880-acre South Platte Park open space area, but feel free to continue farther as time and energy allow.

You'll begin at the Carson Nature Center, located in the heart of South Platte Park. In addition to ample parking and restrooms, the center offers interactive displays, educational programs, public artwork, and several small gardens to entertain you before or after your trek. Turn left on any of the paths leading west toward the river from the center to access the main, paved trail, and begin walking south. You'll quickly come to a junction, where you'll want to turn right and cross the bridge to the west bank of the river. Continue heading southwest on the wide, two-lane trail (the path gets crowded with cyclists at times) lined with rabbitbrush, willows, and cottonwood trees. You'll notice several

Although the main trail is paved for cyclists, there are also several dirt side paths reserved for foot traffic that offer a more natural, serene experience of the lakes and wildlife areas.

designated areas where people can access the river for fishing and paddling sports, as the gentle flow and small rapids here create ideal conditions for both.

You'll soon enter the lakes area, where you'll find several nicely developed observation areas, designed with benches and brick paths encouraging visitors to stay awhile to enjoy the sights and sounds of nature that abound with the surrounding water (read: wildlife habitat). Here you could encounter all kinds of bird species, especially waterfowl, as well

Facing page top: A pleasant observation point overlooking the South Platte River invites you to pause for a moment to enjoy the sights and sounds of nature.
Bottom: The multi-use trail is wide enough for sharing and well-marked for easy navigation, and hugs the riverside for its entirety.

as foxes, coyotes, turtles, and snakes. Be sure to keep an eye on the treetops, too, as the lake names of Eaglewatch and Redtail suggest that birds of prey are common here, too. Continue straight on the paved trail until you reach the Mary Carter Greenway Trailhead, just below the dam of the reservoir.

Here you're welcome to turn around and return to the trailhead on the same route you just walked. Or, if you feel like exploring and conditions aren't too muddy, turn right at the restroom hut and look for a narrow, dirt footpath on the west side of Eaglewatch Lake. This is known as the Lakes Area Trail—a hiker-only path that will give you a closer, quieter experience with the wetland habitat. The dirt path will intercept the main trail in about 1 mile, where you will turn left and then retrace your original route north toward the nature center. After crossing the bridge, however, turn left and stay close to the riverbank as you pass the nature center and continue farther north for the second half of this "figure-eight" loop.

North of the nature center, you are now entering a portion of the park known as the "Northern Wildlife Area." A dirt trail splits off to the left of the paved path and disappears into a grove of trees, called the NWA Loop. This hiker-only footpath meanders close to the river's edge, but ultimately ends in the same place as the paved trail, so feel free to venture down this path if you feel the urge (you could also use this as an alternative return route to shake things up a bit). Otherwise, continue on the paved trail as it winds its way north toward downtown Littleton. You can't see it from here, but Cooley Lake sits to the west of the trail, providing another awesome wildlife habitat, and you'll likely see lots of birds flying overhead in that direction.

When you reach the Reynolds Landing Trailhead, you have come to the northern border of the South Platte Park open space, and the final turnaround point of this hike. Turn around here and retrace your steps back to the Carson Nature Center Trailhead. Of course, the Mary Carter Greenway Trail continues for another 8 miles or so, and then turns into the South Platte River Trail for another 30-plus miles past Denver and into Brighton, so you are also welcome to continue walking until you've had enough, then call a taxi, hop the light rail, or use a rideshare service (such as Uber or Lyft) to return to the trailhead later. Alternatively, there are several bars, restaurants, and coffee shops with direct trail access if you want to take a break and refuel before heading back (recommendations below). Such is the beauty of an urban hiking environment!

MILES AND DIRECTIONS

0.0 Locate the paved trail south of the parking area. Walk behind the nature center and begin hiking southwest on the paved trail.

0.18 Turn right and cross the bridge.

0.26 Continue straight on the main trail.

0.71 Stay left/continue straight on the paved trail.

1.2 Stay right, toward the trailhead.

1.5 Arrive at the Mary Carter Greenway Trailhead, with parking, restrooms, and an informational kiosk. Turn right and follow a dirt footpath around the west side of Eaglewatch Lake.

2.5 Turn left to rejoin the original, paved trail, now moving northeast, and retrace your steps back toward the Carson Nature Center Trailhead.

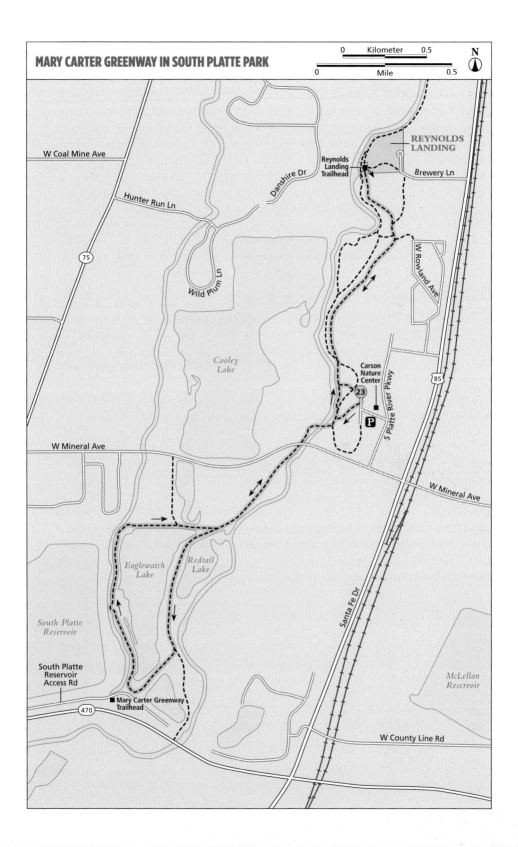

REYNOLDS LANDING

0   Kilometer   0.5

0   Mile   0.5

N

W Coal Mine Ave

Danshire Dr

Reynolds Landing Trailhead

Brewery Ln

Hunter Run Ln

W Rowland Ave

75

Wild Plum Ln

Cooley Lake

Carson Nature Center

85

23

P

W Mineral Ave

W Mineral Ave

S Platte River Pkwy

Eaglewatch Lake

Redtail Lake

South Platte Reservoir

Santa Fe Dr

McLellan Reservoir

South Platte Reservoir Access Rd

470

Mary Carter Greenway Trailhead

W County Line Rd

3.0	Stay left to continue on to the northern part of South Platte Park, for the second half of the figure-eight loop.
3.2	Stay right on the paved path (or turn left to access a dirt footpath that runs parallel to the main trail for the duration of the route).
3.9	Stay left at the roundabout.
4.1	At the Reynolds Landing Trailhead, which marks the northern boundary of South Platte Park, turn around and retrace your path back to the Carson Nature Center Trailhead.
5.0	Arrive back at the trailhead.

LOCAL INTEREST

Breckenridge Brewery & Farmhouse Restaurant: Embodying the epitome of the laid-back Colorado lifestyle, this compound has a sprawling grassy area featuring year-round activities like lawn games, live music, and ice skating to enjoy while you sip the signature suds of one of the state's oldest brewhouses. The adjoining restaurant generates consistently delicious comfort food to boot. 2990 Brewery Ln., Littleton; (303) 803-1380; breckbrew.com/visit/littleton

The Hudson Gardens: This nature and events center offers access to 30 acres of trails, gardens, and ponds year-round, free of charge. It also hosts a full calendar of events and programs, including art classes, Audubon birding walks, and an impressive live music lineup. Don't miss the trailside coffee shop, where cyclists gather after group rides on the Mary Carter Greenway. 6115 S. Santa Fe Dr., Littleton; (303) 797-8565; hudsongardens.org

Alamo Drafthouse Cinema: Located in Aspen Grove, Littleton's premier outdoor shopping, dining, and entertainment development, this "boutique" movie theater boasts seat-side food and beverage service and a lineup of classic and foreign films in addition to new releases. 7301 S. Santa Fe Dr. #850, Littleton; (720) 558-4107; drafthouse.com/denver/theater/littleton

LODGING

Staybridge Suites Denver South-Highlands Ranch: Simple yet sophisticated accommodations featuring rooms with fully equipped kitchens and a spacious outdoor patio with grills, a gas firepit, and stunning views of the foothills. 8211 Southpark Circle, Littleton; (303) 347-9901; ihg.com/staybridge/hotels/us/en/littleton/denll/hoteldetail

24 CHATFIELD FARMS LOOP

A visit to Chatfield Farms is a fun, educational, and therapeutic experience all rolled into one, thanks to a variety of bucolic trails, hands-on agriculture displays, and interesting public art—not to mention glorious gardens of flowers and native plants around every turn.

Elevation gain: 66 feet
Distance: 1.3-mile loop
Hiking time: About 1 hour
Difficulty: Easy
Seasons: Year-round
Trail surface: Paved, dirt
Land status: U.S. Army Corps of Engineers
Nearest town: Littleton
Other trail users: None
Water availability: Yes, at nature center

Canine compatibility: No dogs allowed
Fees and permits: Entrance fee required
Map: Chatfield Farms Map: botanic gardens.org/sites/default/files/file/2020-05/2019chatfieldfarms map_onefellswoop.pdf
Trail contact: Chatfield Farms: (720) 865-3500
Trailhead GPS: N39 33.13' / E105 05.99'

FINDING THE TRAILHEAD

Drive south on Broadway for 3.5 miles to Iowa Avenue. Turn right on Iowa, then left on South Santa Fe Drive. In about 9 miles, turn right onto CO 470 West. Exit onto Wadsworth Boulevard in about 3 miles. Turn left on Wadsworth, then right on Deer Creek Canyon Road. Turn left into the Chatfield Farms entrance, then left into the parking lot. (Denver Botanic Gardens at Chatfield Farms: 8500 W. Deer Creek Canyon Rd., Littleton)

WHAT TO SEE

The Denver Botanic Gardens at Chatfield Farms, located in Littleton, is a lovely place not only to hike but also to learn about western landscapes, agriculture, and history. Visitors of all ages will find something to pique their interest on this 700-acre oasis nestled at the base of the foothills: find a moment of Zen as you work your way through a lavender labyrinth; get nose-to-nose with horses, chickens, and pigs on the historic Hildebrand homestead; watch urban farmers at work in the fields; or immerse yourself in nature with a stroll around an untamed wetlands preserve. This hiking route will lead you through each of these experiences and more in just 1 hour, although you could easily while away an entire afternoon exploring the numerous side trails and gardens more thoroughly.

Start by walking west out of the visitor's center toward the expansive fields of the site's 7-acre working farm. Stroll down the lane lined with fields of flowers, herbs, fruits, and vegetables, which are tended to and shared with members of the Community Supported Agriculture program, one of the organization's many projects to provide more fresh, local produce to underserved plates in some of Denver's "food desert" neighborhoods. Some products are sold at local farmers' markets, especially bouquets of flowers from the "Cut Flower Garden." Also grown in this area are hundreds of heirloom iris flowers, which you'll find blooming in May and June, as well as an orchard of fruit trees.

The Deer Creek Natural Area offers a remote, serene look into untamed riparian and wetland habitats, where you can observe wildlife and enjoy mountain views.

At the end of the fields you'll enter the Hildebrand Ranch area. Listed on the National Register of Historic Places, the site is a close replica of the homestead that was established here in the mid-1800s near the banks of Deer Creek, and features several restored structures including a dairy barn, originally built in 1918, and a schoolhouse, built in 1874. The exhibit also houses live farm animals. Turn left in front of the produce wash station and continue southeast on the paved trail, heading into the Deer Creek Natural Area.

The path winds around a children's play fort before entering a more secluded, woodland area. Don't miss the unique log "hotel" for bees on the left as you move deeper into the forest. You'll walk through a riparian restoration "garden" before emerging from the shaded corridor at a cluster of buildings, including a yurt and the Green Farm Barn, a popular wedding venue. Look closely and you'll find several small gardens tucked around the buildings, including the unique "Survival Garden" full of edible plants. The field to the south is the location for a corn maze and pumpkin patch in the fall—one of the facility's most popular seasonal events (others include a lavender festival in August and a summer butterfly pavilion).

Beyond this complex you will venture into a serene nature preserve, called the Deer Creek Natural Area, where a small network of narrow, dirt footpaths wander around a wide swath of rustic wetland, riparian, and woodland habitats. Keep a keen eye out for

Right: You'll find an array of interesting curiosities along the trail like this unique bee hotel, used to educate visitors about the importance of pollinator populations.
Left: Although most of the gardens go dormant in the winter months, there are plenty of colorful plants and active wildlife to experience.

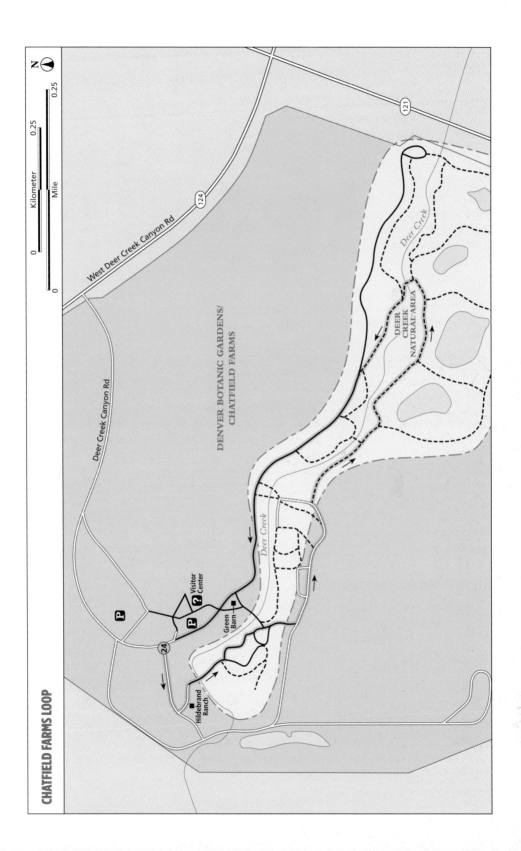

CHATFIELD FARMS LOOP

At the Hildebrand Ranch section of the park, you'll meet all kinds of furry and feathered friends.

signs of wildlife activity, like nests crafted from twigs and leaves in the tree branches, and tree stumps stripped smooth by the gnawing of beavers. Eventually you'll find yourself back on the pavement, near the back side of the event complex. Soon thereafter you'll saunter through the Prairie Garden, featuring native plants that thrive in low-moisture environments, delivering you back at the visitor's center to complete the loop.

MILES AND DIRECTIONS

0.0 Locate the trail northwest of the visitor's center and begin hiking west.

0.08 Turn left.

0.26 Turn left.

0.35 Continue straight.

0.42 Turn right onto the dirt path.

0.55 Stay left.

0.64 Stay left.

0.75 Stay left.

1.2 Continue straight.

1.3 Arrive back at your starting point.

LOCAL INTEREST

Waterton Tavern: This remote neighborhood spot specializes in "Cold Beer & Big Burgers" in a modern yet cozy sports bar atmosphere. 8361 N. Rampart Range Rd., Littleton; (720) 362-2337; watertontavern.com/index.html

Virgilio's Pizzeria & Wine Bar: Named "Colorado's Best Pizza" by *USA Today* for its commitment to fresh ingredients—the Italian-born owner-operator grows his own tomatoes and makes every batch of sauce from scratch. 10025 W. San Juan Way, Littleton; (303) 972-1011; ilovepizzapie.com

LODGING

Chatfield State Park Campground: Complete your immersion in nature by sleeping under the stars along the lakefront at Chatfield State Park. Open year-round with full hookups, group campsites, and coin-operated shower and laundry facilities available. 11500 N. Roxborough Park Rd., Littleton; (303) 791-7275; cpw.state.co.us/placestogo/parks/Chatfield/Pages/Camping.aspx

25 PINEY CREEK TRAIL— PINEY CREEK TRAILHEAD TO LARKSPUR PARK

Distance and incline add adventure to this mellow segment of the Piney Creek Trail, which has everything you could ask for in a (sub)urban hike: a well-maintained pathway, nice landscaping offering plentiful habitat for wildlife, and convenient recreational facilities along the way.

Elevation gain: 218 feet
Distance: 10.7 miles out and back
Hiking time: About 3.5 hours
Difficulty: Easy
Seasons: Year-round
Trail surface: Paved
Land status: Arapahoe County Open Spaces
Nearest town: Centennial
Other trail users: Cyclists, joggers
Water availability: Yes, at Trails Recreation Center

Canine compatibility: Yes, on leash
Fees and permits: None
Map: Explore Arapahoe County Bike and Trail Map: arapahoegov .com/DocumentCenter/View/6219/ Explore-Arapahoe-Trails-Map?bidId=
Trail contact: Arapahoe Parks & Recreation District: (303) 269-8400
Trailhead GPS: N39 36.63' / E104 48.48'

FINDING THE TRAILHEAD

From downtown Denver, drive south on I-25 for 10 miles to I-225 North. In 4 miles take exit 4 onto CO 83/Parker Road, then stay right. Turn left on Orchard Road in about 3.5 miles, then turn right into the parking lot.

WHAT TO SEE

Stretching about 10 miles between the suburban cities of Centennial and Aurora southeast of Denver, this popular neighborhood route alternates between the super urban (road crossings and tunneled underpasses) and the somewhat rural (ponds, creeks, and other protected wildlife areas), with plenty of suburban recreational amenities in between (parks, playgrounds, golf courses, and recreation centers). It is mainly utilized by residents of the surrounding neighborhoods for jogging, walking the dog, cycling, and family outings. The Piney Creek Trail wasn't always a proverbial "walk in the park," however, as the path was created around the historic Smoky Hill Trail, a dangerous and desolate wagon route traveled by hopeful settlers from the east flocking to Colorado during the gold rush in the mid–1850s.

This hike features just the 5-mile section of trail located in Centennial, from Piney Creek Trailhead to Larkspur Park, for a more manageable distance, but feel free to continue on toward the Aurora section if you feel up to it. The trail technically originates in the fee-based Cherry Creek State Park, but we'll start at the Piney Creek Trailhead instead. Located just a few miles east of the park, this trailhead is free to access and has plenty of parking from the adjacent shopping center. Heading east on the paved trail, you'll first travel along a wide greenway, handsomely landscaped with native plants and

This well-maintained, sun-drenched path is perfect for a wintertime outing—even the morning following a large, wet snowstorm.

grasses, with the Piney Creek riparian corridor on your right and Orchard Road on your left. At the end of this straightaway you'll come to the Trails Recreation Center, a large development with a skate park, indoor pool, and fitness programs for all ages (you can also use the restrooms and get water here if needed). Although you are moving east, you are actually hiking up a slight incline on the way out, and will appreciate the downhill slant on your way back when you are more tired.

Continue on the trail following Orchard Road until you come to South Tower Road, then follow the trail as it takes a sharp right turn and heads south to cut through Piney Creek Hollow Park. After the park the trail passes through several residential neighborhoods and around several major roadways—be sure to use the underpasses and crosswalks as available for safe navigation through these urban obstacles. You'll also pass by the Saddle Rock Golf Course before turning right once again, now moving southeast away from the roadway into a quieter, more residential region.

Although you can occasionally snag some shade under the gnarled cottonwoods scattered throughout the route, for the most part this trail is fully exposed. Here the intense Colorado sunshine can be your friend or foe, depending on the season—in the winter, the snow melts off the pavement quickly, providing access year-round; in the summer, this path bakes with little vegetation to help cool it. The creek helps, but there is no direct access to the water on this hike. When you arrive at Larkspur Park, you have reached the eastern border of the city of Centennial. You can turn around here and retrace your path back to the trailhead, or continue east into the city of Aurora for several more miles.

A walk alongside Piney Creek wasn't always so pleasant; the route was once used by westward wagons and commonly known as the "starvation" trail.

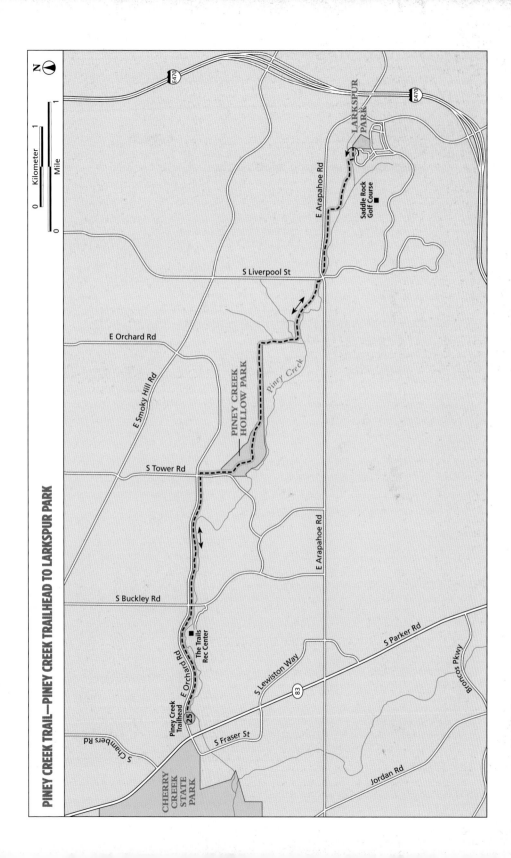

PINEY CREEK TRAIL—PINEY CREEK TRAILHEAD TO LARKSPUR PARK

N

0   Kilometer   1

0   Mile   1

E470

LARKSPUR PARK

E Arapahoe Rd

Saddle Rock Golf Course

S Liverpool St

E Orchard Rd

E Smoky Hill Rd

PINEY CREEK HOLLOW PARK

Piney Creek

S Tower Rd

E Arapahoe Rd

S Buckley Rd

The Trails Rec Center

S Chambers Rd

E Orchard Rd

Piney Creek Trailhead

25

S Fraser St

S Lewiston Way

83

S Parker Rd

Broncos Pkwy

Jordan Rd

CHERRY CREEK STATE PARK

MILES AND DIRECTIONS

0.0 Locate the trail on the northeast corner of the parking lot, beyond the information kiosk.

0.74 Stay left to bypass the recreation center.

1.7 Continue straight.

2.0 Turn right.

2.5 Arrive at Piney Creek Hollow Park. Continue straight.

3.3 Turn right.

3.5 Continue straight.

4.2 Continue straight, through the underpass.

4.7 Turn right.

5.2 Follow the paved trail as it jogs right, then left.

5.3 Turn around at Larkspur Park and retrace your steps back to the trailhead.

10.7 Arrive back at the Piney Creek Trailhead.

LOCAL INTEREST

Doug's Day Diner: Located in the Piney Creek Square shopping center, this casual Colorado diner/chain is everything a local eatery should be: The food is homemade (try the breakfast burrito), the service is friendly, and the price is right. 15444 E. Orchard Rd., Centennial; (720) 870-6228; dougsdiner.com

LODGING

Fairfield Inn & Suites Denver Aurora/Parker: Fresh, affordable accommodations near the Southlands shopping center, with an indoor pool and outdoor patio. 24192 E. Prospect Ave., Aurora; (303) 928-7500; marriott.com/hotels/travel/denas-fairfield-inn-and-suites-denver-aurora-parker

WEST METRO

As you drive west from downtown, the high-rises shrink into the rearview mirror and the landscape widens as you head toward the suburban cities of Wheat Ridge and Lakewood. It's amazing what a difference a few miles can make, as within mere minutes you'll notice more trees, bigger skies, and a more mountainous backdrop. These areas are coveted for their proximity to big-city amenities and urban luxuries while also offering easy access to an abundance of trails, parks, lakes, and creeks.

Clear Creek is one of the main geographic features in this region, and most of the hikes detailed here will lead you to it at some point. In fact, this waterway is a key thread

West Denver trails are known for their wide-open spaces, abundance and variety of trees, and creekside corridors.

A hopeful prospector sifting through the sandy sediment of Clear Creek looking for a flash of gold.

in the monumental Peaks to Plains Trail project, an ambitious recreational plan aimed at connecting the Denver International Airport to the Continental Divide. Although it is still years away from full realization, in the following pages you'll find information about the few sections that are completed, as they prove to be some of the nicest, most beautiful trails in the area.

Clear Creek is also where some of the state's first gold nuggets were discovered, leading to the gold rush of the 1850s and ultimately the founding of the original Denver City. As you stroll along its grassy banks, imagine plunging your hands into the icy water for hours on end, hoping to strike it rich. You might not have to use your imagination too much, however, as prospecting is still a popular pastime and there are areas along these trails where you might see someone trying their hand at this unique hobby.

Although West Denver is best known for its outdoor offerings, it's also heralded for its dynamic, multicultural communities where you will discover vibrant public artwork, authentic ethnic shops and restaurants, and enriching attractions like theaters, museums, and historic landmarks, providing a plethora of urban activities to enjoy before or after your hike.

26 CLEAR CREEK TRAIL— WHEAT RIDGE GREENBELT

The Wheat Ridge Greenbelt is a popular neighborhood destination for recreation and scenery, with the paved Clear Creek Trail offering endless water views, and boasts one of the Denver area's best-kept secrets for bird-watching.

Elevation gain: 90 feet
Distance: 6.7 miles out and back
Hiking time: About 2.5 hours
Difficulty: Easy
Seasons: Year-round
Trail surface: Paved, dirt, boardwalk
Land status: City of Wheat Ridge
Nearest town: Wheat Ridge
Other trail users: Cyclists, joggers
Water availability: Yes, at trailhead
Canine compatibility: Yes, on leash

Fees and permits: None
Map: Wheat Ridge Greenbelt & Clear Creek Trail Map: rootedinfun.com/DocumentCenter/View/94/Wheat-Ridge-Greenbelt—Clear-Creek-Trail-Map?bidId=
Trail contact: Wheat Ridge Parks & Recreation: (303) 231-1300
Trailhead GPS: N39 46.52' / E105 05.91'

FINDING THE TRAILHEAD

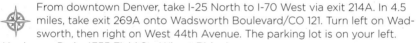

From downtown Denver, take I-25 North to I-70 West via exit 214A. In 4.5 miles, take exit 269A onto Wadsworth Boulevard/CO 121. Turn left on Wadsworth, then right on West 44th Avenue. The parking lot is on your left. (Anderson Park: 4355 Field St., Wheat Ridge)

WHAT TO SEE

The majority of the city of Wheat Ridge's 300 acres of open space is encompassed in the Wheat Ridge Greenbelt, which flanks about 5 miles of Clear Creek in northwest Denver. The area features several parks, lakes, and both paved and unpaved trails for recreationists. It is also recognized as one of the most pristine riparian habitats in the Denver area, providing a safe haven for some 300 species of migratory birds. Multiple access points with parking, restrooms, picnic pavilions, and water fountains are conveniently available every few miles, so you can hop off and on as necessary—as this route is on the longer side.

Start by walking west on the paved trail located on the south side of Anderson Park, home to the Carnation Festival, one of Colorado's oldest events, which has been celebrating Wheat Ridge's title of "Carnation Capital of the World" since the 1960s. The trail meanders along the creek underneath the shady cover of towering mature cottonwood trees. Be aware of cyclists whizzing by, as this section of trail intersects with the city's Central Bikeway. Most cyclists using this popular commuter route have good trail etiquette and will notify you of their presence by ringing a bell on their handlebars before passing. You can also help share the trail by staying to the right on the path and walking single file when necessary.

When you reach Kipling Street, follow the paved path to the left—first crossing over a bridge before winding its way through an underpass, which will safely deliver you to

The Wheat Ridge Greenbelt is especially beautiful in the fall when its corridor of mature cottonwood trees turn a brilliant yellow hue.

Bass Lake features a wildlife viewing boardwalk for a closer look at the wetland ecosystem.

The west end of the greenbelt offers a quieter, dirt path for foot traffic only.

the other side of the road. Turn right in front of the Wheat Ridge Recreation Center and rejoin the main trail on the north side of the parking lot. This section of trail is more open, with almost no trees for shade. However, in recent years the city has made an effort to "Revive the Greenbelt" by planting thousands of new trees, shrubs, and other plants to help improve the native ecosystem. On your left is a small pasture housing "working goats"—yet another progressive city project that uses livestock to help maintain its open space areas and reduce invasive weeds.

Next you'll come to Prospect Park. Cross the bridge to the left and continue hiking west. Here you'll notice an abundance of birdlife as you approach a lakes district: Prospect and Tabor Lakes are to the north, while Bass and West Lakes are to the south. Look for cormorants drying their wings on the banks, flocks of bathing ducks and geese, and herons fishing among the cattails. These waters are also stocked with catfish, bass, and bluegill for fishing.

When you reach the Youngfield Street Trailhead, follow the trail under I-70 to discover the Arapahoe Bar Gold Panning Park, where you might catch a glimpse of a modern prospector hard at work with their tools in the creekbed. Gold panning is one of Colorado's oldest pastimes, and it can still be enjoyed in some designated areas. The Clear Creek corridor is where Colorado's first gold nuggets were discovered, causing an influx of settlers to the territory in the 1850s, and is one of the most popular areas for rock hounding still today. You will turn around here, but the Clear Creek Trail continues on for about 5 miles into the city of Golden. Plans to eventually continue the trail all the way up to the Continental Divide are already in the works as part of the Peaks to Plains Trail project.

When you arrive back at Bass Lake, turn right and follow a path around the south side of the conservation area, where you'll find a wooden boardwalk providing a closer view of the marsh, which is home to hundreds of bird species. Afterward, turn right and retrace your steps back to the trailhead. You could also use the hiker-only footpath

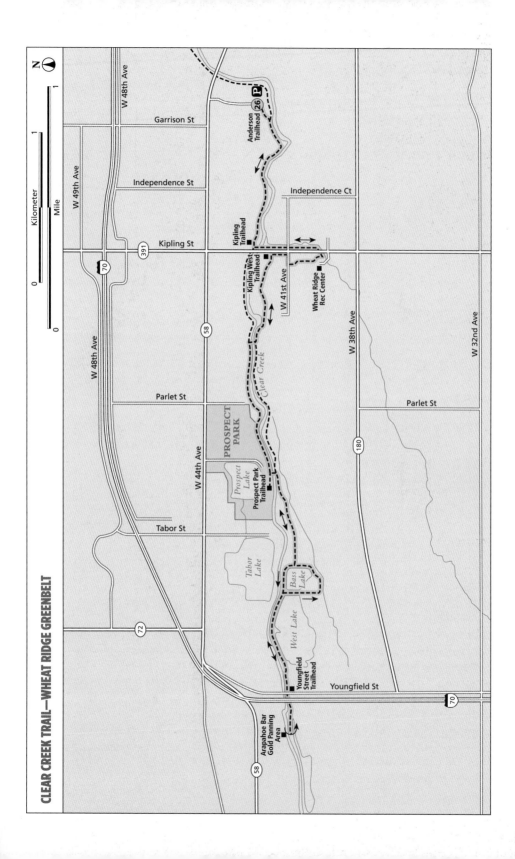

CLEAR CREEK TRAIL—WHEAT RIDGE GREENBELT

N

Kilometer
Mile

W 48th Ave

Garrison St

W 49th Ave

Independence St

Independence Ct

Kipling St

Anderson
Trailhead

Kipling
Trailhead

Kipling West
Trailhead

W 41st Ave

Wheat Ridge
Rec Center

Clear Creek

W 38th Ave

W 32nd Ave

W 48th Ave

Parlet St

Parlet St

PROSPECT
PARK

W 44th Ave

Prospect
Lake

Prospect Park
Trailhead

Tabor St

Tabor
Lake

Bass Lake

West Lake

Youngfield
Street
Trailhead

Youngfield St

Arapahoe Bar
Gold Panning
Area

that travels along the south of the creek to experience the more serene, bike-free side of the greenbelt on your return route instead. Feel free to poke down any side trails you discover that lead to the water to get a closer look at the riparian ecosystem this area is known for. If you opt for the dirt trail, simply turn left when you reach the Miller Trailhead to rejoin the paved path, which will then lead you back to the trailhead.

MILES AND DIRECTIONS

0.0 Locate the paved trail on the south side of Anderson Park and begin hiking west.

0.5 Turn left and follow the trail as it crosses over a bridge and through an underpass to safely cross Kipling Street.

0.87 Turn right, cutting through the parking lot of the Wheat Ridge Recreation Center.

1.0 Turn right, then left, toward the Kipling West Trailhead. Continue hiking west.

1.5 At the junction, turn right to cross the bridge, continuing on the paved path.

2.0 At Prospect Park, cross the bridge on your left and continue west on the main trail.

2.5 Turn right to walk around the north side of Bass Lake.

2.7 Continue straight, toward West Lake.

3.3 Turn around at Arapahoe Bar Gold Panning Area and retrace your steps to Bass Lake.

3.8 Stay right to flank Bass Lake to the south.

4.2 At the end of the wooden boardwalk, turn right and retrace your steps back to the trailhead.

6.7 Arrive back at the trailhead.

LOCAL INTEREST

Grammy's Italian Goodies: This family owned and operated spot serves huge pizza slices, hot and cold sandwiches, pasta dishes, and a wide variety of homemade baked goods, and was featured on the Food Channel's *Diners, Drive-Ins and Dives* in 2020. 4601 Harlan St, Wheat Ridge; (303) 422-0380; grammysitaliangoodies.com

Discovery Tap House: A community-oriented beer bar with a wide variety of Colorado crafts on tap, plus a full calendar of events and specials, like game nights and food truck visits. 4990 Kipling St. #7, Wheat Ridge; (720) 532-0944; discoverytaphouse.com

LODGING

Holiday Inn Express & Suites Wheat Ridge Denver–West: Clean, affordable, no-frills hotel located near the Kipling West Trailhead with an outdoor pool and complimentary breakfast. 10101 W. 48th Ave., Wheat Ridge; (303) 424-8300; ihg.com/holidayinnexpress/hotels/us/en/wheat-ridge/denwr/hoteldetail?cm_mmc=GoogleMaps-_-EX-_-US-_-DENWR

Prospect RV Park: Seventy RV sites featuring full hookups, restrooms, and Wi-Fi located adjacent to the Wheat Ridge Greenbelt, offering a serene natural setting and easy access to lakes and trails. Monthly rates available. 11600 W. 44th Ave., Wheat Ridge; (303) 424-4414; prospectrv.com

27 CROWN HILL PARK LOOP

Centered around a large lake, this 279-acre suburban oasis harbors a trove of bird-watching opportunities, thanks to a gated wildlife sanctuary on the northwest corner of the park, as well as numerous benches and picnic tables perched overlooking the lake.

Elevation gain: 38 feet
Distance: 2.8-mile double-loop
Hiking time: About 1 hour
Difficulty: Easy
Seasons: Year-round
Trail surface: Paved, dirt
Land status: Jefferson County Open Space Parks and Trails
Nearest town: Wheat Ridge
Other trail users: Cyclists, equestrians
Water availability: Yes, at trailhead

Canine compatibility: Dogs allowed in Crown Hill Park on leash; no dogs allowed in wildlife sanctuary area
Fees and permits: None
Map: Jefferson County Open Space Map of Crown Hill Park: jeffco.us/DocumentCenter/View/9367/Crown-Hill-Park-Map?bidId=
Trail contact: Jefferson County Open Space: (303) 271-5925
Trailhead GPS: N39 45.02' / W 105 06.13'

FINDING THE TRAILHEAD

From Denver, travel west on US 6 for about 4 miles. Take the exit toward CO 121 North/Wadsworth Boulevard and turn right. In about 2 miles, turn left on West 26th Avenue. The trailhead parking lot will be on your right in about 1 mile, at the intersection with Garland Street. (Crown Hill Garland Trailhead: 9357 W. 26th Ave., Wheat Ridge)

WHAT TO SEE

Located in the heart of Wheat Ridge, what was once property of the neighboring Olinger Crown Hill Cemetery is now a neighborhood destination for scenic walks, bird-watching, picnics, and horseback riding. Ten miles of paved and dirt trails are woven around Crown Hill Lake offering an array of route combinations: The Outer Loop Trail is a 2.5-mile paved path that follows the park's perimeter, while the 1.2-mile Lake Loop Trail hugs the grassy banks of the lake. Both trails provide access to the 0.5-mile Kestrel Pond Trail, which is reserved for foot traffic only as it loops around an Urban National Wildlife Refuge, where numerous bird species can be spotted. This route is customized to give you a taste of each of these main trails, but feel free to venture down any of the numerous dirt connector paths you'll come across, too, if you wish to explore the park further.

From the Garland Trailhead you'll start out heading west, moving clockwise around the lake. Right away you'll come to another trailhead, which is primarily used for horse trailer parking and equestrian access, and notice the hilly topography of the mountains in the distance. As you round the southwest corner of the park and begin hiking north along Kipling Street, you'll pass through a meadow of prairie grasses dotted with cottonwood and pine trees, and catch your first glimpse of the white "Tower of Memories" mausoleum presiding over the cemetery across the lake, located along the park's eastern border.

A view of the Crown Hill Cemetery across the lake.

Just before reaching the park's northwest corner, you'll arrive at one of the gated entrances to the wildlife preserve. If restrictions allow, turn right to enter the preserve (this area is accessible to pedestrians only, and is closed seasonally from March through June to protect bird populations). Once inside, you're greeted by a gravel pathway lined with cottonwood trees. This short loop will guide you around Kestrel Pond, a protected wetlands area aptly named, as it provides a safe harbor for migratory birds of all kinds (visit jeffco.us/1207/Crown-Hill-Park to view a checklist of birds that have been spotted in the park, and see if you can find any yourself). In addition to bird-watching, this corner of the park offers a supremely serene hideout for those seeking a quiet, meditative moment.

At the southeast corner of the sanctuary is a boardwalk structure cutting through a sea of cattails, jutting into the wetlands for optimal viewing. There is also another gate at this end, where you can exit the preserve and access the lake and the Lake Loop Trail. You may take this option, cutting off the northwest corner of the main trail, or you can finish the short loop and rejoin the Outer Loop Trail via the same gate through which you entered the preserve. Turn right onto the main trail to continue on your journey around the perimeter of Crown Hill Park.

You'll soon come to a junction with an information board. Turn right here to head south toward the lake, flanking the wetlands area and moving from the Outer Loop Trail to the Lake Loop Trail (as usual, you can also continue straight to complete the full Outer Loop Trail, which will continue to hug the perimeter of the park and lead you

An abundance of leafy cottonwood trees make this trail a great choice for autumn.

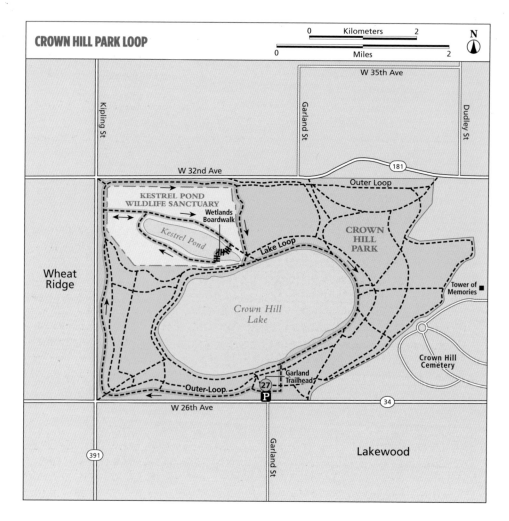

CROWN HILL PARK LOOP

| 0 | Kilometers | 2 |
| 0 | Miles | 2 |

N

W 35th Ave

Kipling St

Garland St

Dudley St

W 32nd Ave

181

Outer Loop

KESTREL POND
WILDLIFE SANCTUARY

Wetlands
Boardwalk

Kestrel Pond

Lake Loop

CROWN
HILL
PARK

Wheat
Ridge

Crown Hill
Lake

Tower of
Memories

Crown Hill
Cemetery

Garland
Trailhead

Outer Loop

27

34

W 26th Ave

391

Garland St

Lakewood

W 26th Ave

straight back to the trailhead). Once you reach the lake, you'll see a viewing platform with spotting scopes provided for magnified bird-watching. There's also a few benches and a picnic pavilion if you are ready to take a break.

Continuing on, you'll see the white tower growing larger in view as you near the cemetery. For an even closer look you can take one of the dirt connector trails east to the outer trail once more. Otherwise, stay close to the lake and enjoy the expansive views over the water and to the hills beyond. When you reach the south side of the lake along 26th Avenue, turn left on any of the connector trails to reenter the trailhead and parking lot.

MILES AND DIRECTIONS

0.0 Locate the trail north of the parking area. Turn left and begin walking west, moving clockwise around the lake on the Outer Loop Trail.

0.38 Follow the trail around the corner to the right, continuing north along Kipling Street.

0.8	Turn right and pass through the gate to enter the Kestrel Pond Wildlife Refuge (pedestrians only). If this area is closed, continue straight on the main trail instead.
1.4	Turn left to exit the wildlife refuge area through the same gate you entered from.
1.6	Follow the main trail around the corner to the east, now moving parallel to West 32nd Avenue.
2.0	Turn right at the information sign to head south toward the lake, moving from the Outer Loop Trail to the Lake Loop Trail.
2.2	When you reach the lake observation point, turn left to continue moving clockwise around the lake.
2.8	Turn left into the Garland Trailhead parking area.

LOCAL INTEREST

Little Brazil: Locally owned and operated Brazilian cafe featuring authentic dishes like black bean stew, beef empanadas, and fried plantains. 10081 W. 26th Ave., Wheat Ridge; (303) 427-2270; littlebrazilco.com

Danny's Carnation Restaurant: A family-friendly diner whipping up a large variety of breakfast skillets, deli sandwiches, burgers, Mexican classics, homemade desserts, and pretty much everything in between. Specials available for children, seniors, and early birds. 1395 Wadsworth Blvd., Denver; (303) 238-3045; dannyscarnationrestaurant.com

Colorado Plus Brewpub: Showcasing a wall lined with fifty-six taps pouring some of the best craft beers in the state, including a few of their own creation, this is a one-stop shop for sampling suds. Soak it up with something off the well-rounded, scratch-made food menu. 6995 W. 38th Ave., Wheat Ridge; (720) 353-4853; coloradoplus.net

LODGING

Cozy Denver West Getaway (Airbnb): Located on the northeast corner of Crown Hill Park, this modern duplex is outfitted with all the comforts of home, like a fully equipped kitchen, fenced-in yard, and Hulu Plus. Wheat Ridge; airbnb.com/rooms/46987357?federated _search_id=5f62e306-32b3-434b-859e-df1756d77992&source_impression_id=p3_1612 735119_%2FZBwPUsa%2BBNRNcpE

Holiday Inn Express & Suites: Conveniently located off I-70 with an outdoor pool and a complimentary breakfast. 10101 W. 48th Ave., Wheat Ridge; (303) 424-8300; ihg .com/holidayinnexpress/hotels/us/en/wheat-ridge/denwr

28 **40 WEST ARTLINE**

Make like Dorothy and follow the "green line" through parks, down alleyways, and along Denver's infamous Colfax Avenue for an urban hike unlike any other, where you'll discover colorful murals, modern art galleries, and interactive installations in every nook and cranny of this edgy arts district.

Elevation gain: 96 feet	**Water availability:** No
Distance: 4.5-mile multi-loop	**Canine compatibility:** Yes, on leash
Hiking time: About 1 hour	**Fees and permits:** None
Difficulty: Easy	**Map:** 40 West Artline Route Map:
Seasons: Year-round	40westartline.org/map
Trail surface: Paved	**Trail contact:** 40 West Arts: (303)
Land status: City of Lakewood	275-3430
Nearest town: Lakewood	**Trailhead GPS:** N39 44.73' / E105
Other trail users: Cyclists, joggers	03.74'

FINDING THE TRAILHEAD

From downtown Denver, drive west on Colfax Avenue for about 3.5 miles, then turn right onto Harlan Street. Park at the Edgewood Civic Center and Library complex on the right.

WHAT TO SEE

Developed by the 40 West Arts District—a nonprofit organization and one of twenty-six state-certified Creative Districts in Colorado—the ArtLine is a thoughtfully designed tour of community parks, artist galleries, local landmarks, and more than seventy displays of public artworks scattered throughout the neighborhoods along West Colfax Avenue in Lakewood. Perhaps one of the most infamous streets in town, Colfax is the longest commercial street in America and a part of US 40, also known as "America's Main Street" because it stretches from California to New Jersey. Originally lined with the mansions and museums of Denver's Victorian elite, it later devolved into an area known for its more risque offerings, such as dive bars and prostitutes. More recently, much effort has been put forth to revitalize the thoroughfare to its deserved splendor while also celebrating its gritty charm.

To start, park at the Edgewater Civic Center and Library complex and look for the green line painted on the sidewalk along Harlan Street, and begin walking south. You'll soon come to Walker-Branch Park, where you'll turn left and follow the line through *Stegoskel*, one of three installations inspired by the stegosaurus dinosaur, fossils of which were first discovered near Lakewood. Continue down Harlan Street, making sure to look down from time to time, as the route features a variety of "ground murals," many of which encourage you to play a movement game. Next you'll come to Mountair Park, the heart of the Two Creeks neighborhood, with a ball field, garden, musical "playground," and several statues. Follow the line as it winds around the Mountair Park Community Farm and moves parallel to the light rail tracks. Notice the glittering light catchers hanging on the chain-link fence and the beautification of the utility boxes between the tracks,

The "green line" tour takes you through some of the Denver area's up-and-coming neighborhoods, featuring urban artwork along the way.

and marvel at how these local artists have creatively transformed even the most unlikely urban surfaces into masterpieces.

After passing Lamar Station, both a light rail stop and an upcoming pocket neighborhood of its own accord, turn right on Lamar Street. Follow the green line to the west side of the street when you come to the roundabout with the award-winning puzzle piece installation, *Connected*, then look for a red park bench featuring bronze statues in tribute to the former fire station nearby. The next block is lined with apartment buildings brilliantly awash with murals of flowers and weeds, titled *Wild Urban Medicine*.

When you come to Colfax Avenue, cross to the north side of the street at the stoplight, then turn left. You'll take a quick jaunt along the busy roadway, where you'll see several more murals as well as the pink tower of Casa Bonita, one of Denver's most storied restaurants. Turn right on Pierce Street, heading north through a much quieter residential area, where you'll enjoy more fence art displays and murals leading up to the campus of the Rocky Mountain College of Art + Design, before turning left on 17th Avenue. The trail passes through a spacious, serene greenway dotted with mature trees offering plentiful shade and greenery on the way to Aviation Park, the smallest of the three parks featured on the route.

Next you'll head toward the actual West 40 Arts District, located in and around 16th Avenue between Teller and Pierce Streets. This little maze of alleyways houses a collection of contemporary galleries, industrial workshops, and street art, which open their

doors to the public during special events like First Friday art walks and summertime art festivals. Near the corner of 16th and Teller, beyond the large, circular *Aztec Maze* ground mural, sits the Benchmark Theatre, which hosts a variety of live performances and artist workshops, adding to the district's diverse roster of creative styles.

After poking around the funky arts district, return to Colfax Avenue. From here you can retrace your original path for an inverse viewpoint of the trail and its outdoor decor, or you can take Colfax back to the trailhead on Harlan Street directly as a shortcut.

MILES AND DIRECTIONS

0.0   Locate the trail north of the parking area on Harlan Street, just south of 20th Street, and begin walking south on the green line.

0.15 Turn left into Walker-Branch Park.

0.24 Turn right, following the path along the perimeter of the park.

0.46 Turn left to continue on the main trail.

0.73 Turn left on 14th Avenue.

0.92 Turn right to travel southwest through Mountair Park.

1.0   Turn left at the community garden.

1.1   Turn right to travel west along the train tracks.

1.5   Turn right on Lamar Street.

1.8   Turn left on Colfax Avenue.

2.1   Turn right on Pierce Street.

2.3   Turn left on 17th Avenue.

2.4   Turn right on Reed Street.

2.5   Walk diagonally down the path toward Aviation Park.

2.6   Turn left to walk clockwise around the park, then retrace your steps back to Reed Street.

2.9   Turn right on Reed Street.

3.1   Turn right on West 16th Avenue.

3.2   Turn left on Teller Street.

3.3   Turn left, cutting through a parking lot lined with galleries, making your way back to 16th Avenue.

3.4   Turn right on 16th Avenue.

3.5   Turn right on Reed Street, then left on Lakewood Place.

3.6   Turn right on Pierce Street.

3.7   Turn left on Colfax Avenue.

4.2   Turn left on Harlan Street.

4.5   Arrive back at the trailhead.

Facing page top: The ArtLine takes you through three charming neighborhood parks featuring urban amenities like community gardens, skate parks, and art installations.
Bottom: Located in front of the 40 West Arts District gallery space, this Aztec-inspired ground mural pays homage to the largely Latin population that resides in the surrounding area.

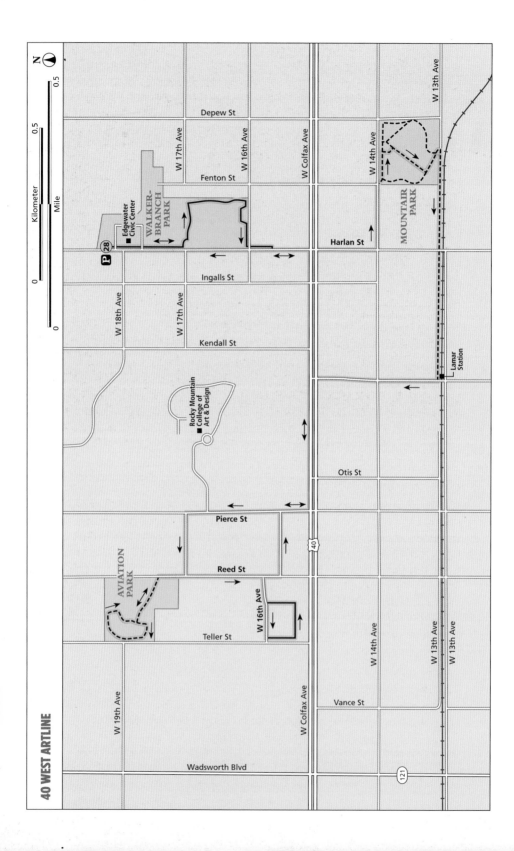

The public artwork on display throughout the hike is as edgy as its main thoroughfare, Colfax Avenue, which was once recognized by *Playboy* magazine as one of the "wickedest" streets in America.

LOCAL INTEREST

WestFax Brewing: Located in the Lamar Station Plaza just steps away from the ArtLine, this community-oriented operation serves "liberated" beers in a modern taproom with an outdoor patio. Try the 40 West IPA with something scrumptious from the food truck rotation. 6733 W. Colfax Ave., Lakewood; (303) 233-3742; westfaxbrewingcompany.com

Casa Bonita: This zany complex feels more like a Mexican resort than a restaurant, which is why it's been heralded as one of the country's leading "roadside attractions" for more than forty years. Dine under palm trees, tiki huts, and a 30-foot indoor waterfall while watching a full schedule of live performances, from cliff divers to gunfighters. 6715 W. Colfax Ave., Lakewood; casabonitadenver.com/about

LODGING

The Perry Hotel: Stylish, apartment-style accommodations with all the comforts of home within walking distance to a slew of Denver hot spots, trails, and landmarks. 1525 Perry St., Denver; (720) 923-7870; ecghotels.com/the-perry-hotel

29 BELMAR PARK LOOP

This urban park in the western suburb of Lakewood celebrates community with multi-use trails, wildlife observation areas, public artwork, and charming outdoor exhibits to educate visitors about the city's history and heritage.

Elevation gain: 35 feet
Distance: 1.7-mile lollipop loop
Hiking time: About 45 minutes
Difficulty: Easy
Seasons: Year-round
Trail surface: Paved, dirt
Land status: City of Lakewood
Nearest town: Lakewood
Other trail users: Cyclists, equestrians
Water availability: No

Canine compatibility: Yes, on leash
Fees and permits: None
Map: Lakewood Trail Explorer (interactive map): egis.lakewood.org/apps/LakewoodTrailExplorer/
Trail contact: City of Lakewood Community Resources Department: (303) 987-7800
Trailhead GPS: N39 42.21' / E105 05.13'

FINDING THE TRAILHEAD

From downtown Denver, take US 6 West to the Wadsworth Boulevard exit. Drive south on Wadsworth Boulevard for about 1.5 miles, then turn right on Ohio Avenue. Park at the Lakewood Heritage Center, located on the left side of the road. (Belmar Park: 801 S. Wadsworth Blvd., Lakewood)

WHAT TO SEE

Situated at the heart of Lakewood, this urban park combines nature, history, and entertainment in 150 acres of open space, creating a true sense of the term "community center." This short perimeter trail encircles meadows, lakes, and numerous smaller social trails, offering a pleasant and scenic respite for humans, plants, and animals alike. The park also houses a unique outdoor museum made up of historic buildings for an informative walking tour through the ages of Lakewood's history, as well as a small pavilion where outdoor concerts draw spectators from the surrounding neighborhoods.

You'll begin your hike at the heritage center, located near the southeast corner of the park, and walk clockwise around the lake. Take a stroll down the promenade through the "Colfax Hub" lined with historic buildings relocated from around Denver that were originally built in the 1940s to 1960s era. Turn left at the roundabout to poke around additional clusters of historic structures, including the "Belmar Hub," which features houses, barns, and outbuildings preserved from the summer estates of Denver's early elite who came to the lake to escape the city heat around the turn of the century, such as Molly "Unsinkable" Brown and the founder of the *Denver Post* newspaper. The red barn is the most modern building in the collection; it was built in the 1990s to store the heritage center's collection of antique farm equipment.

Walk west from the roundabout on the paved trail to begin hiking clockwise around the lake. There are several dirt paths throughout the park that you are welcome to explore to add more mileage to your route, but the main trail hugs the perimeter of the park, offering continuous views of the lake and foothills, as well as a glimpse into the

Despite a reputation for having "bad" winters, the Denver area receives over 300 sunny, blue-sky days, making hiking enjoyable year-round.

Located on the west side of Denver, Lakewood is known for its views of the foothills and abundance of open space.

Belmar Park has an extensive trail network of both paved and dirt paths for hiking, jogging, cycling, and horseback riding.

surrounding residential neighborhoods, many of which are actually small farm properties. As such, the park is a popular destination for equestrians, who mostly stick to the inner dirt trails.

In addition to the museum collections, the park is nicely developed with an abundance of benches, gazebos, bronze statues, and wildlife observation points dispersed throughout. Follow your nose to check out as many of these curiosities as you wish, keeping in mind that the thrill of urban hiking is about discovering beauty in unexpected places, like finding a secluded spot to watch the ducks dive in a small pond, or enjoying a piece of public artwork that you would normally rush past without noticing. As long as the lake is on your right-hand side, you're going in the correct general direction. A few notable installations include a "natural" playground created with boulders, ropes, and other things to climb located in the northwest corner of the park, and a serene wetlands boardwalk tucked into the northeast corner of the lake.

On the homestretch of trail on the east side of the park, you'll come across a side path leading to a boardwalk jutting over the lake, offering a view of a rookery on a small island. Here you have the chance to watch a number of waterfowl and migratory birds nesting, fishing, and mating (on a visit in late fall I was pleasantly surprised to spot a pair of enormous herons roosting in a tree almost directly over the trail). Once you've spent some time on the observation deck, return to the main trail and continue walking south back toward the heritage center to complete the hike.

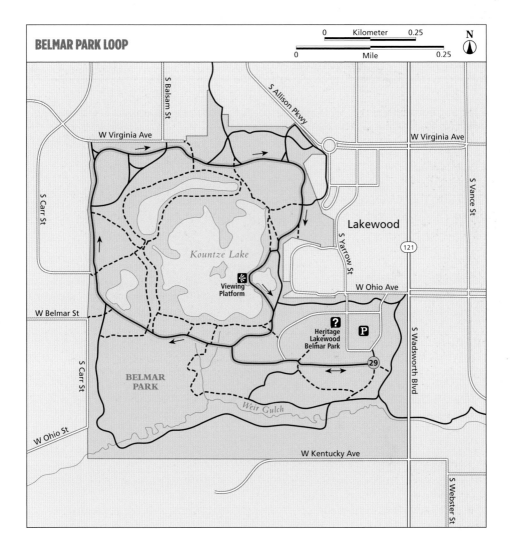

BELMAR PARK LOOP

MILES AND DIRECTIONS

0.0 Starting in front of the heritage center on the southeast corner of the parking lot, begin walking down the wide promenade lined with historic buildings.

0.1 When you reach the roundabout, turn right on the paved path and head toward the lake.

0.24 Turn left to move clockwise around the lake on the paved (or dirt) path.

0.5 Stay on the paved path as it turns north. Continue following this trail around the perimeter of the park, with the lake on your right-hand side.

1.2 Turn right down a smaller footpath leading to a viewing platform over the lake.

1.3 Continue south on the main path.

1.4 Turn left to return to the parking area.

1.7 Arrive back at the trailhead.

LOCAL INTEREST

Farmhouse Thai: Lakewood is known for its variety of ethnic food restaurants, and this family owned and operated exotic eatery features some particularly hard-to-find authentic menu items. 98 S. Wadsworth Blvd., Lakewood; (303) 237-2475; farmhouse thaieatery.com

Kickin Chicken: This no-fuss fried chicken kitchen features a small menu with big flavors. 275 S. Union Blvd., Lakewood; (303) 989-0197; kickinchickenrestaurant.com

LODGING

Hyatt House Denver/Lakewood at Belmar: Located in a modern outdoor shopping center just minutes from Belmar Park. Full kitchens available. 7310 W. Alaska Dr., Lakewood; (303) 922-2511; hyatt.com/en-US/hotel/colorado/hyatt-house-denver-lakewood-at-belmar/denxl

30 BEAR CREEK GREENBELT

The Bear Creek Greenbelt often gets overshadowed by its big brother to the west—the massive, 2,600-acre Bear Creek Lake Park—but this smaller open space offers a nice network of trails that meander through a pretty streamside corridor, providing a more peaceful, rustic hiking experience.

Elevation gain: 59 feet
Distance: 3.6-mile loop
Hiking time: 1–2 hours
Difficulty: Easy
Seasons: Year-round
Trail surface: Paved, dirt
Land status: City of Lakewood
Nearest town: Lakewood
Other trail users: Cyclists, joggers
Water availability: Yes

Canine compatibility: Dogs must remain on leash
Fees and permits: None
Map: Lakewood Trail Explorer (interactive map): egis.lakewood.org/apps/LakewoodTrailExplorer
Trail contact: City of Lakewood Community Resources Department: (303) 987-7800
Trailhead GPS: N39 39.90' / E105 05.70'

FINDING THE TRAILHEAD

From downtown Denver, drive west on US 6 to Wadsworth Boulevard South. Turn left off the exit, then right on US 8/Morrison Road in approximately 3.7 miles. Turn left on South Estes Street in less than 1 mile, then left into the parking area in 0.5 mile. (2900 S. Estes St., Lakewood)

WHAT TO SEE

Located about 5 miles west of Denver, Lakewood is the fifth-largest city in Colorado and boasts some 107 miles of multi-use trails across 7,200 acres of open space. The Bear Creek Greenbelt comprises 379 acres, the majority of which exist between Wadsworth Boulevard and Kipling Street. Keep in mind that there are several different paths, some dirt and some paved, that crisscross each other frequently, making precise wayfinding somewhat maddening (they are the Stonehouse Trail, the Bear Creek Trail, and the Bear Creek Greenbelt Trail). But don't despair—embrace the opportunity to "get lost," and trust that they all generally lead to the same place.

Begin your hike on the north end of the parking area, where you'll see the historic Stone House. Built around 1860 and added to the National Register of Historic Places around 1976, this quaint structure is now used as an event venue, and also provides a nice place to rest thanks to its serene garden surroundings. Walking southeast, you'll pass a fishing pond before coming to the main trail(s). Turn left on the first dirt footpath you come to, flanking the pond (this is technically known as the Bear Creek Greenbelt Trail, which travels north of the creek). Although the majority of the Bear Creek corridor is a riparian forest habitat, lined with cottonwood trees and willows, this portion of the trail features a wetlands area, where you can see fish swimming, waterfowl bathing, and clusters of cattails swaying along the water's edge. About one-half mile into your trek you have the opportunity to veer down to the creekside on your right for an up-close look

The Bear Creek Greenbelt receives plentiful sunshine, making it an ideal year-round destination.

at the riparian zone. Be sure to pause from time to time and look for birds camouflaged in the foliage, or just listen to the water trickling over the rocks.

When you reach Wadsworth Boulevard, follow the corner to the right to meet up with the paved trail (technically the Bear Creek Trail). Here the trail temporarily moves south and west, ascending away from the creek and into a prairie zone. There are no trees to shade the trail on this side, offering an unobstructed view of the mountains to the west. You'll likely recognize the lumpy dens of prairie dogs all around you, and might even spot a few of these creatures scurrying around.

About 2 miles into the hike you'll cross South Estes Street, near the parking area, continuing west. Here the stream is a bit wider and slower, creating a nice, protected place for wildlife to hang out. Follow the trail over an arched footbridge to the right, making sure to stop on top for a different perspective of the creek (which can rise quite high in the "spring" runoff season—and can actually last until July—so tread carefully). When you reach Kipling Street, follow any of the trails around the corner to the right, now heading east back toward the trailhead. The trails in this area get especially thin and winding, obscured by an abundance of willows and greenery. They also have a tendency to become very muddy, so try to stay as "high and dry" as possible, to protect the trail as well as your hiking shoes. You'll cross back over South Estes Street once more to reenter the parking area from the west.

The greenbelt offers a variety of dirt, gravel, and paved paths to explore.

All trails lead to water, and bird-watching opportunities to boot.

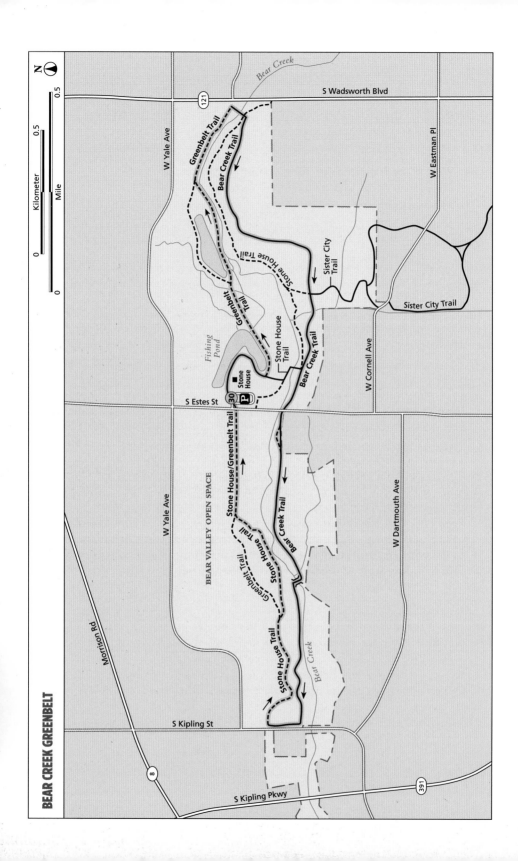

BEAR CREEK GREENBELT

N

Kilometer
0   0.5

Mile
0   0.5

Bear Creek

S Wadsworth Blvd

121

W Yale Ave

W Eastman Pl

Greenbelt Trail

Bear Creek Trail

Stone House Trail

Sister City Trail

Sister City Trail

Greenbelt Trail

Fishing Pond

Stone House

Stone House Trail

Bear Creek Trail

W Cornell Ave

S Estes St

30

P

Stone House/Greenbelt Trail

BEAR VALLEY OPEN SPACE

W Yale Ave

Bear Creek Trail

Greenbelt Trail

Stone House Trail

W Dartmouth Ave

Morrison Rd

Stone House Trail

Bear Creek

S Kipling St

8

Bear Creek

S Kipling Pkwy

391

MILES AND DIRECTIONS

0.0 Locate the trail on the north side of the parking lot, beyond the Stone House building.

0.2 Stay left on the trail, hugging the pond's edge (Bear Creek Greenbelt Trail).

0.34 Continue straight on the dirt path.

0.45 Stay on the path to the right. Another small lake will appear on your left.

0.55 Veer right, downhill to a narrow creekside trail.

0.72 Turn right onto the main trail after ascending from the creekbed.

0.84 Stay right at the fork.

0.93 Before reaching Wadsworth Boulevard, turn right across the creek and continue onto the paved trail (Bear Creek Trail).

1.8 Cross South Estes Street.

2.0 Stay left to continue on the Bear Creek Trail.

2.3 Cross the footbridge on your left.

2.7 Turn right before reaching Kipling Street, rounding the corner to head back east.

3.4 Stay right at the junction.

3.6 Cross over South Estes Street once more to enter the parking area from the west.

LOCAL INTEREST

Granny Scott's Pie Shop: In addition to a dizzying selection of award-winning hand-made pies, you'll also find a full menu of deli-style lunch meals (complete with a slice of pie!). 3333 S. Wadsworth Blvd. #C-107, Lakewood; (303) 986-6240; grannyscotts.com

The Yabby Hut: This family owned and operated casual kitchen specializes in fresh shellfish and build-your-own seafood platters with Cajun flair. Check their homepage for daily specials and a "Fresh Crawfish Status" meter. 3355 S. Yarrow St. #E-131, Lakewood; (303) 985-0231; yabbyhut.com

Front Porch Coffee Shop: Located inside the Bridge Church, this coffeehouse was created to provide a safe, healthy hangout spot for the city's youth, and offers a menu of coffee drinks, breakfast sandwiches, and pastries to be enjoyed on a spacious, sunny patio. 3101 S. Kipling St., Lakewood; frontporchcoffeeshop.com

LODGING

Best Western Denver Southwest: Guests rave about the outdoor pool and unique prehistoric attributes that make the hotel lobby feel more like a natural history museum. 3440 S. Vance St., Lakewood; (303) 989-5500; bestwestern.com/en_US/book/hotels-in -lakewood/best-western-denver-southwest/propertyCode.06170.html

Private Guest House on Bear Creek (Airbnb): You and your pets are welcome on this secluded ranch, with a deck overlooking the creek and trail. airbnb.com/ rooms/9837846?source_impression_id=p3_1610672856_9ucIXTOdLQwoihmN

A herd of elk hanging out on the front lawn of an apartment complex in Evergreen.

THE FOOTHILLS

The geographic term "foothills" refers to the area between a plains region and a mountain range, a transition marked by a change in terrain from a relatively flat, arid landscape to one with rolling hills, rocky soil, and less vegetation. With the elevation gain you'll notice that the sun feels stronger and the air feels thinner, contributing to that infamous "Rocky Mountain high" as you gradually ascend to literally dizzying heights.

In the Denver area the foothills are located to the west, and include the towns of Morrison, Evergreen, and Golden, all of which are within an approximately 30-minute drive from downtown. This region is known for its scenic beauty, access to outdoor recreation, and rich mining history, all of which can be experienced during a drive along the

Coniferous trees and grassy meadows are common characteristics of Denver foothills hiking trails.

40-mile Lariat Loop National Scenic Byway. The route is designed to showcase some of Denver's top historic landmarks and cultural attractions in just a few hours by car—while also offering access to creeks, parks, and a slew of trails—including several that are featured in the following pages—making for a fantastic day trip from the city.

In addition to its city parks and trails, Denver also manages some 14,000 acres of open space spanning three counties, including twenty-two conservation areas. The uber-unique Denver Mountain Parks system was founded in 1914 and features soaring mountain peaks, alpine lakes, historic structures, unparalleled wildlife habitat, and miles upon miles of rugged trails. A few of the highlights of these city-owned treasures are detailed in this section, although there are many, many more to explore.

In the foothills, everything is more unpredictable, from the weather to the wildlife. In the summertime you could experience lighting strikes in the middle of broad daylight and snow in July. In the winter, you'll discover snow-covered trails and frozen lakes and streams. Thanks to the higher altitude, exposure to intense sunshine and the accompanying risk of dehydration are practically guaranteed year-round. Here the trails are steeper and rockier, and you will share them with rattlesnakes, black bears, and mountain lions—things to be aware of, but not afraid of.

Despite being decidedly less urban than those in other chapters, these foothills hikes offer a taste of the alpine environment Colorado is famous for without venturing too far from the city. What qualifies them as "urban" is that they still offer basic amenities such as trailhead restrooms and proximity to restaurants and other activities. If you're up for the challenge, be sure to pack extra water, several layers, and your sense of adventure, and head for the hills.

31 RED ROCKS TRAIL/ MORRISON SLIDE LOOP

Venture toward the funky mountain town of Morrison to experience the beauty and challenge of one of the most iconic trails in the Denver area, located just around the corner from the equally iconic Red Rocks Amphitheatre.

Elevation gain: 541 feet
Distance: 5.5-mile lollipop loop
Hiking time: About 1.5 hours
Difficulty: Difficult, due to elevation gain and uneven terrain
Seasons: Year-round
Trail surface: Dirt
Land status: Jefferson County Open Space Parks and Trails
Nearest town: Morrison
Other trail users: Mountain bikers

Water availability: No
Canine compatibility: Yes, on leash
Fees and permits: None
Map: Jefferson County Open Space Matthews Winters Park Map: jeffco .us/DocumentCenter/View/9376/ MatthewsWinters-Park-Map?bidId=
Trail contact: Jefferson County Open Space: (303) 271-5925
Trailhead GPS: N39 41.67' / E105 12.29'

FINDING THE TRAILHEAD

From downtown Denver, take US 6 West for about 9 miles to I-70 West. From I-70, take exit 259 toward Morrison. Turn left on CR 93, then right on CR 73. The parking lot for the Matthews-Winters Trailhead is on the left.

WHAT TO SEE

Although this hike does offer a glimpse into Red Rocks Park—home to the famed Red Rocks Amphitheatre and part of the unique Denver Mountain Parks system—the main trailhead is located at the Matthews-Winters Park in Golden. Although you can't see the concert venue itself from the trail, it is surrounded by the same stunning geology and views that the amphitheatre is known for, and it's dramatically different from any other hike in this book: rust-colored dirt underfoot, dramatic rock formations towering above, and desert plants abound. A few different trails have been combined to create a nice loop tour of the area, and due to the challenging terrain you'll have the option to omit portions that might be too steep for your liking. No matter which path you choose, you'll enjoy awesome scenery you won't soon forget.

The trail begins on the south side of the parking area, on a path called "Village Walk." This is a wide, rolling path that heads up a hillside dotted with juniper trees. It will lead you past a historic cemetery consisting of a few crumbling remnants of the once-bustling mining supply town from the 1860s called Mount Vernon. Soon after the cemetery you'll turn right onto the Red Rocks Trail. After about a mile of winding dirt path surrounded by spiky yucca plants and scraggly juniper trees, you'll come to another trail junction. Take the switchback to the left to stay on the main trail, which will begin to get narrower, rockier, and steeper as it wraps around a hill covered in boulders.

At the top you'll be rewarded with sweeping views of meadows punctuated with remarkable rock formations, two of which make the "walls" of the Red Rocks

The mineral-rich soil and dramatic rock formations of the foothills region make for stunning scenery just outside Denver.

The rocky terrain dotted with sagebrush and larger-than-life views make the area surrounding Red Rocks Park feel like a scene out of a Western film.

Amphitheatre, which help create unparalleled acoustics coveted by musical artists around the globe. From here you have the choice of turning around and retracing your steps back to the trailhead, or conquering a steep portion of switchbacks, visible below and to the northwest, which turns the hike into a challenging yet rewarding loop.

Continuing on, you'll first descend the hill you're standing on toward the trail junction at the bottom of the gulch. If you turn left you'll end up at the smaller, southern trailhead in Red Rocks Park. Instead, turn right to climb the "Morrison Slide." Plan to take plenty of breaks as you make your way up the rocky hairpin turns of this section of trail (to catch your breath, but also to take in the dizzying views). When you reach the top, you can celebrate because it's all downhill from here (mostly!) Here the trail levels out, providing a pleasant stroll with 360-degree views. To the east lies Dinosaur Ridge, an area boasting some of the best-preserved dinosaur tracks in the country. On a clear day you can see the city of Golden in the distance to the north. Continue on the Morrison Slide Trail as it descends another series of switchbacks on the north side of the hill. Stay right at the bottom and follow signs to return to the trailhead via the Red Rocks Trail.

Ocher-colored paths cut through the rocky landscape in Matthews-Winters Park.

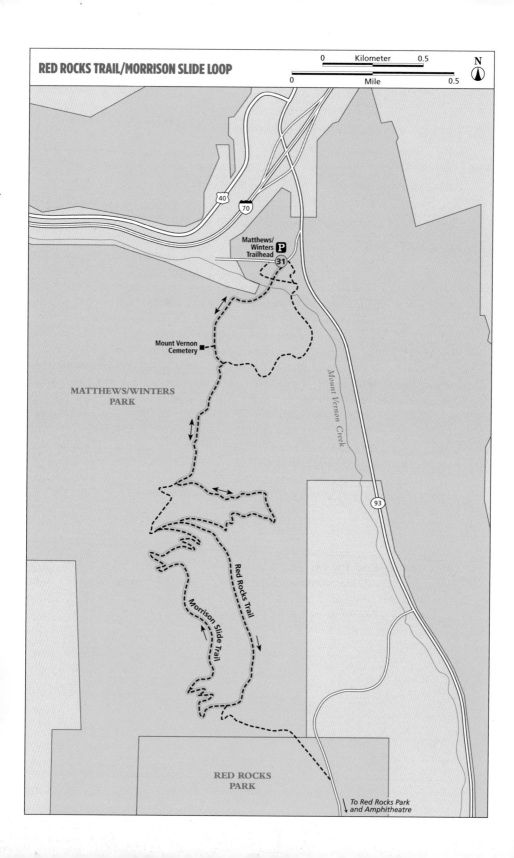

RED ROCKS TRAIL/MORRISON SLIDE LOOP

0 — Kilometer — 0.5

0 — Mile — 0.5

N

Matthews/
Winters
Trailhead **P**
31

Mount Vernon Cemetery

Mount Vernon Creek

**MATTHEWS/WINTERS
PARK**

40
70

93

Red Rocks Trail

Morrison Slide Trail

**RED ROCKS
PARK**

*To Red Rocks Park
and Amphitheatre*

MILES AND DIRECTIONS

0.0   Locate the trail south of the parking lot. Cross a small footbridge to begin walking on the Village Walk Trail.

0.45 Turn right onto the Red Rocks Trail.

0.86 Turn left to continue on the Red Rocks Trail.

1.6   Take a sharp left to continue up the Red Rocks Trail.

2.3   At the bottom of the gulch, stay right toward the Morrison Slide Trail.

3.8   Turn right, then stay left, continuing on the Red Rocks Trail.

4.6   Stay right on the Red Rocks Trail.

5.0   Turn left and return to the trailhead via the Village Walk Trail.

5.5   Arrive back at the parking area.

LOCAL INTEREST

Red Rocks Beer Garden: With an award-winning 2,000-square-foot outdoor patio, craft beer on tap, and pizza, it really doesn't get much more "Colorado" than this. 116 Stone St., Morrison; (208) 861-7873; redrocksbeergarden.com

Ship Rock Grille: Located in the Visitor Center at Red Rocks, you can take a stroll through the Red Rocks Hall of Fame before enjoying a meal with an unobstructed view of the surrounding landscape. Great for special occasions as well as a post-hike cocktail. Call ahead for reservations, as hours and access vary from day to day based on the amphitheatre schedule. 18300 W. Alameda Pkwy., Morrison; (303) 697-4939; redrocksonline.com/plan-your-visit/eat-drink

Dinosaur Ridge: Just down the road from the trailhead is the site of some of the best-preserved dinosaur tracks in the country. Learn about Colorado's prehistoric era at the exhibit hall, take a guided walking tour with a geologist, or practice using archaeological tools at a hands-on dig site. 16831 W. Alameda Pkwy., Morrison; (303) 697-3466; dinoridge.org

LODGING

Origin Hotel Red Rocks: This boutique hotel is the official hotel of Red Rocks Amphitheatre, with hip amenities like outdoor firepits and complimentary mountain bikes that make every guest feel like a rock star. 18485 W. Colfax Ave., Golden; (303) 215-0100; originhotel.com/hotels/red-rocks

32 EVERGREEN LAKE LOOP

Evergreen Lake is the crown jewel of this popular foothills town thanks to a plethora of year-round, family-friendly activities and stunning mountain forest scenery.

Elevation gain: 57 feet
Distance: 1.3-mile loop
Hiking time: About 30 minutes
Difficulty: Easy
Seasons: Year-round
Trail surface: Paved, boardwalk, dirt
Land status: Denver Parks & Recreation (Denver Mountain Parks)
Nearest town: Evergreen
Other trail users: Joggers
Water availability: Yes, summer only

Canine compatibility: Yes, on leash
Fees and permits: None
Map: Denver Mountain Parks Dedisse Park Map: denvergov.org/content/dam/denvergov/Portals/747/documents/ParkArt/Dedisse_Park Map.pdf
Trail contact: Evergreen Park & Recreation District: (720) 880-1300
Trailhead GPS: N39 37.89' / W105 19.936'

FINDING THE TRAILHEAD

From downtown Denver, drive west on US 6 for 9.5 miles to I-70 West. After continuing another 9.5 miles on 1-70, take exit 252 onto Evergreen Parkway/CO 74. In 7 miles, turn right onto Upper Bear Creek Road, then take the first left into the park. (Evergreen Lake House: 29612 Upper Bear Creek Rd., Evergreen)

WHAT TO SEE

Located about 35 minutes from Denver, the town of Evergreen is popular for its rustic charm, homestead heritage, and semi-rural feel. Thanks to a rich mining history that left behind a slew of historic ranches and landmarks, the area is one of the main attractions along the Lariat Loop National Scenic Byway. Situated at the heart of town, Evergreen Lake anchors the 55-acre Dedisse Park—listed on the National Register of Historic Places and part of Denver's unique mountain parks system—making a great base camp from which to explore. This easy loop trail offers a nice introduction to the park and its mountain forest landscape.

Start out at the Evergreen Lake House, located on the northeast side of the parking lot. This handsome log structure is a popular space for events and serves as the epicenter for year-round water sports, including a rink for ice skating and pond hockey in the winter. Heading north on the trail, moving clockwise around the lake, you'll first zigzag through a wetlands area on a boardwalk. Here you can enjoy up-close encounters with a variety of waterfowl, fish, and plant life. When you reach the end of the boardwalk, continue on a paved path to the right to flank the north side of the lake, parallel to Bear Creek Road. This side of the lake offers a beautiful view of the lake house, access to the water's edge, and park benches to sit on. At the eastern end of this stretch rises the Evergreen Dam, built in 1928, which created the lake as an attraction for outdoor recreation as well as to help control flooding in the neighborhoods downstream. Follow the trail around the back side of the dam, where you'll find the pleasant surprise of a bronze cowboy statue and park bench hiding in the shadows behind the concrete slab.

The northwest corner of the lake features a well-constructed boardwalk hovering over a wetlands area full of fish, bird, and plant life.

Evergreen Lake is a hub of year-round outdoor activity, including hiking, ice skating, and sledding in the winter months.

Continuing on, now heading south-southwest on the trail, you'll have a full view of the layers of mountain terrain beyond the lake house—a perfect backdrop for watching the sunset. Here the trail is a tad more narrow and rugged with a dirt surface and a few small hills to navigate (if you are hiking in the winter, be mindful of slick spots). On this side, the trail passes beneath a neighborhood of cottages and cabins on a hill overlooking the lake, some of which are more than one hundred years old. You'll also walk past another historic structure: a wooden shelter that was originally built to function as a warming hut and now houses the Evergreen Nature Center and Audubon. This rustic outpost features hands-on wildlife displays, a program calendar of field trips around the lake, and information about birding in the area.

Soon after passing the nature center and boat ramp, you'll arrive back at the trailhead parking lot. If you wish to spend more time basking in the phenomenal scenery and mountain air, there are tables and grills available here for a post-hike picnic.

MILES AND DIRECTIONS

0.0 Locate the trail near the Lake House on the northeast corner of the parking area and begin walking north along a boardwalk through a small wetlands area, moving clockwise around the lake.

0.7 Follow the trail up and over the dam to the right.

1.3 Arrive back at the parking area.

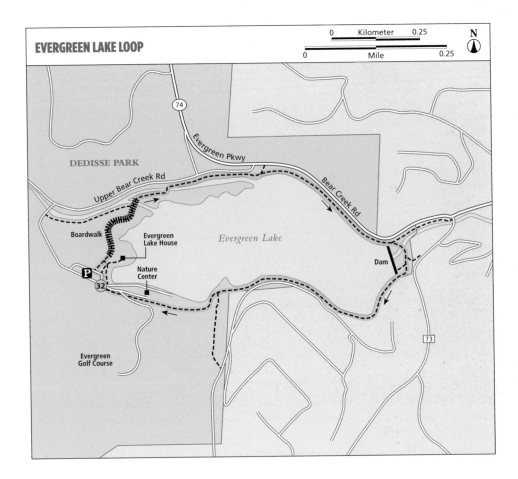

DEDISSE PARK

74

Evergreen Pkwy

Upper Bear Creek Rd

Bear Creek Rd

Boardwalk

Evergreen Lake House

Evergreen Lake

Dam

P

Nature Center

32

73

Evergreen Golf Course

LOCAL INTEREST

Murphy's Mountain Grill: This local gem gets rave reviews for its outdoor patio, rustic decor, and well-executed menu of comfort food favorites with Southwestern flair. 27906 CO 74, Evergreen; (720) 524-8621; murphysmountaingrill.com

Lariat Lodge Brewing: Evergreen's award-winning cornerstone brewery features a rooftop patio overlooking Bear Creek, a full bar, and a food menu. 27618 Fireweed Dr., Evergreen; (303) 674-1842; lariatlodgebrewing.com

Little Bear Saloon: This renowned restaurant and concert venue features classic Western decor and a full schedule of live entertainment. Belly up to the bar and prepare to witness some mountain town shenanigans. 28075 CO 74, Evergreen; (303) 674-9991; littlebearsaloon.com

LODGING

Colorado Bear Creek Cabins: A small collection of well-appointed, pet-friendly log cabins just steps from the creek with full kitchens and outdoor patios. 27400 CO 74, Evergreen; (303) 674-3442; coloradobearcreekcabins.com

33 NORTH BISON OVERLOOK AT GENESEE PARK

This fun roadside attraction is a great place for a quick leg stretch en route to the mountains or the airport—and no matter your age, saying hello to the buffalo herd never gets old.

Elevation gain: 158 feet
Distance: 1.8 miles out and back
Hiking time: About 30 minutes
Difficulty: Easy
Seasons: Year-round
Trail surface: Paved
Land status: City and County of Denver
Nearest town: Golden
Other trail users: Cyclists
Water availability: No

Canine compatibility: Yes, on leash
Fees and permits: None
Map: Denver Mountain Parks Genesee Park Map: denvergov .org/content/dam/denvergov/ Portals/747/documents/ParkArt/ Genesee_ParkMap.pdf
Trail contact: Denver Mountain Parks: (720) 865-0900
Trailhead GPS: N39 42.93' / W105 18.551'

FINDING THE TRAILHEAD

From downtown Denver, take US 6 West for about 10 miles to I-70 West. After driving for about 8.5 miles on I-70, take exit 253 onto Moss Rock Road, then turn right. Turn right onto Stapleton Road, then left into the parking area. (Beaver Brook Trailhead: 27661 Stapleton Dr., Golden)

WHAT TO SEE

The largest and oldest park in Denver's unique mountain parks system is home to one of the last remaining bison herds in America, and was monumental in saving these gentle giants from extinction due to overhunting in the early 1900s. In partnership with the Denver Zoo, this "conservation herd" descended from wild bison and is part of a program that aims to return them to tribal lands across the country. Although this short trail is technically known simply as the "I-70 Bike Route," it is most popular with pedestrian passersby who stop to gawk at the buffalo habitat. It's an easy and entertaining hike for tourists and families with children, but even longtime locals will enjoy the scenic stroll alongside sweeping meadows dotted with enormous conifers and snow-capped mountain views.

While you could also start from the Genesee Park trailhead on the eastern end of the trail, this route is designed to send you uphill first and downhill on the way back, which is slightly easier on the legs and lungs. Other benefits of the Beaver Brook Trailhead include restrooms and a nice display of information boards that explain important things to know before your hike, such as the history of the Denver Mountain Parks system and what the difference is between a buffalo and a bison (spoiler alert: Although both words are commonly used interchangeably to describe the creatures you are about to see, "bison" is the correct scientific term).

You'll start out walking east with the meadow on your left and the interstate on your right. Yes, this trail hugs the highway closely and there is a fair amount of traffic noise,

Although the bison is not Colorado's official state animal, it is the beloved mascot of the University of Colorado, whose resident buffalo "Ralphie" charges the field before each football game.

but despite this the trail is surprisingly beautiful and peaceful. Right away you'll come to a roundabout "observation point" with park benches and interpretive signage about the area's history, buffalo (or bison) factoids, and a park map. If you're lucky the herd will be gathered in this corner of the park, and you'll get a glimpse right off the bat. The herd is sometimes relocated to another pasture across the freeway via an underground tunnel, but you will still have a good view either way (if this is the case, you can drive over to the Bison Meadow Trailhead in Genesee Park after your hike for a closer look).

This easy out-and-back trail dips and winds around the enclosure on a wide, paved path alongside a tall fence through an area known as Genesee Park. Besides the bison,

With mountain views, mature pine forests, and a resident bison herd, this roadside trail is not to be underestimated.

An observation area near the trailhead provides a shady place to rest while learning about the history and importance of the American bison.

the most striking features you'll notice in the meadow are the towering ponderosa pine trees—some of which are as old as the park itself, which was founded in 1912. You'll continue to climb gradually uphill until the trail dead-ends at South Mount Vernon Country Club Road, where you'll find another observation point and some picnic tables. After catching your breath, simply turn around and retrace your steps back to the trailhead. Although the herd may roam wherever it pleases throughout the park, it is often found gathered in this eastern corner (be sure not to get too close to the fence, as the buffalo have been known to charge). On the return journey you'll enjoy a leisurely downhill trek with fantastic mountain views.

MILES AND DIRECTIONS

0.0 Locate the paved trail on the southeast corner of the parking area, beyond the restrooms, and begin walking east toward the observation roundabout.

0.12 Stay left and continue hiking east.

0.91 When you reach the road, turn around and retrace your steps back to the trailhead.

1.8 Arrive back at the Beaver Brook Trailhead.

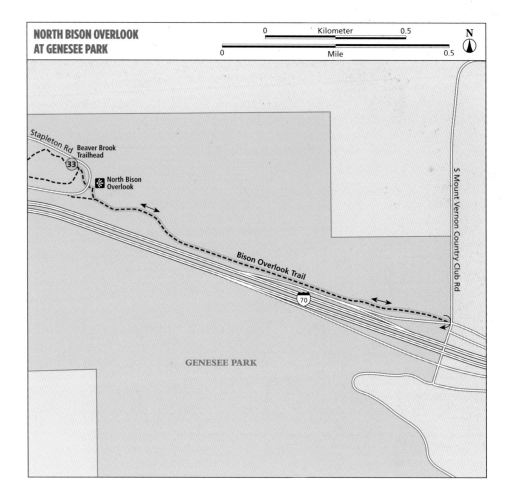

NORTH BISON OVERLOOK AT GENESEE PARK

LOCAL INTEREST

Chart House Restaurant: Enjoy a bird's-eye view of the mountains at this upscale chain, perched on a hill overlooking Genesee Park, which specializes in seafood. Seats on the fireside patio are especially coveted during happy hour and sunset times. 25908 Genesee Trail Rd., Golden; (303) 526-9813; chart-house.com/location/chart-house-genesee-co

Lariat Loop National Scenic Byway: Genesee Park is one of many historic landmarks located along this 40-mile driving route that leads you through the foothills towns of Golden, Evergreen, and Morrison in just a few hours. lariatloop.org

LODGING

Chief Hosa Campground: Share a sunrise with the resident bison herd munching hay across the meadow from your tent at this 58-acre campground located in Genesee Park. The historic campground offers direct trail access, coin-operated shower facilities, full RV hookups, and proximity to modern conveniences like grocery stores and movie theaters. 27661 Genesee Dr., Golden; (303) 526-1324; denvergov.org/Government/Departments/Parks-Recreation/Parks/Chief-Hosa-Campground

34 LOOKOUT MOUNTAIN PARK LOOP

The region's iconic Lookout Mountain invites you to fill your lungs with fresh mountain air, learn about the region's native flora and fauna, and visit a few notable historic landmarks, including the grave site of one of the West's most legendary figures, William "Buffalo Bill" Cody, on this rocky trek above 7,000 feet in elevation.

Elevation gain: 498 feet
Distance: 3.0-mile lollipop loop
Hiking time: 1–2 hours
Difficulty: Moderate, due to altitude and terrain
Seasons: Year-round
Trail surface: Dirt
Land status: City and County of Denver
Nearest town: Golden
Other trail users: Mountain bikers
Water availability: No
Canine compatibility: Yes, on leash

Fees and permits: There is no fee to access the trail or nature center; however, a fee is required to enter the museum.
Map: Lookout Mountain Park Map: denvergov.org/content/dam/denvergov/Portals/747/documents/ParkArt/LookoutMtn_ParkMap.pdf
Trail contact: Denver Parks & Recreation: (720) 913-1311
Trailhead GPS: N39 43.868' / W105 14.481'

FINDING THE TRAILHEAD

From downtown Denver, take I-70 West to exit 256 for Lookout Mountain. Turn right at the end of the exit ramp, then make a quick left onto US 40. Veer right onto Paradise Road and left onto Charros Drive. Turn right on Lookout Mountain Drive and drive about 4 miles, passing the nature center entrance and following signs toward the Buffalo Bill Museum and Trailhead. Turn left into the parking area.

WHAT TO SEE

Located less than 30 minutes from downtown Denver, Lookout Mountain Park is the perfect place to get a taste of what more mountainous terrain entails. Despite being a popular training ground for competitive runners and cyclists (be sure to drive cautiously and watch for both on the narrow, winding approach to the park), the area also offers gentle dirt paths through shady forests of ponderosa pine trees with scenic views of the nearby city of Golden, and some notable attractions—including the Buffalo Bill Museum, an interactive nature center, and the Boettcher Mansion, an architectural gem included on the National Register of Historic Places—making it an immensely pleasant and interesting place to spend a few hours outside the city.

This hike starts and ends at the Buffalo Bill Trailhead (where a museum and cafe can also be found), with the Lookout Mountain Nature Center situated at the halfway point. With additional parking available at both the nature center and the Lookout Mountain Trailhead, located 0.5 mile south of the museum, there are a few different ways you can structure your visit. This route, however, ensures you have access to urban amenities (restrooms, water, interactive entertainment) throughout. Although you can complete

Left: The Buffalo Bill trail starts out in a shaded forest and ascends to a montane meadow dotted with enormous pine trees, displaying panoramic views the whole way.
Keep an eye out for Abert's squirrels, a unique breed with a charcoal-colored coat that thrives in coniferous areas.

the hike in about an hour, allow at least an extra hour (or two) to explore and learn along the way. You can check out the museum area either before or after your hike, but don't miss the sweeping views from the grave site itself, which is positioned at the highest point of Lookout Mountain at about 7,372 feet in elevation.

From the parking area, head south on the Buffalo Bill Trail, a hilly, hiker-only path that leads to a display of interpretive signs pointing out significant geographical and geo-logical points of interest within view. Following signs to the Lookout Mountain Trail, you'll continue downhill on a dirt path and across a footbridge lined with cottonwood trees. Be sure to stay left at the fork and follow this rocky, multi-use trail uphill (watch for mountain bikers). Though this section is short, at this point you'll likely start to feel your legs and lungs start to burn as your blood cells begin to register the high altitude. Near the top of this hill you'll find a picnic table where you can catch your breath and catch a glimpse of downtown Golden framed by spiky pine boughs.

Next, you'll cross the road (cautiously, as there is no crosswalk provided) to enter the Lookout Mountain Preserve and Nature Center. The 100-acre sanctuary features a nature center with hands-on activities for kids and 2.5 miles of wide, flat trails that mean-der through groves of aspen and ponderosa pines and sprawling meadows of tall native grasses. These hiker-only trails—aptly named the Forest and Meadow Loop Trails—offer impressive solitude and wildlife despite their accessibility. While strolling through this section you'll find massive pine cones scattered along the trail, and hopefully spot the surprising charcoal-colored coats of the Abert's squirrel, a unique member of the squirrel family that subsists on pine cones and needles as opposed to acorns and nuts.

This short loop around a meadow behind the nature center is open to hikers only and offers a peaceful place to observe wildlife like deer, foxes, and squirrels.

West of the nature center, you'll see a handsome historic lodge known as the Boettcher Mansion. Originally constructed as a summer retreat for Denver businessman Charles Boettcher in 1917, the well-preserved structure was added to the National Register of Historic Places in 1984 for its notable Arts and Crafts architectural design, and is now primarily used as a venue for private events.

From here you'll walk back across the road and head back the way you came, this time descending the rocky, heart-pumping hill.

MILES AND DIRECTIONS

0.0 Begin at the Buffalo Bill Trailhead, located at the north side of the parking lot.

0.25 Head south, downhill, until you reach the interpretive lookout point. Continue straight, following signs toward the Lookout Mountain Trail.

0.5 Stay left at the fork and continue uphill on the Lookout Mountain Trail.

0.75 At the top of the hill, turn left to cross Colorow Road and enter the Lookout Mountain Preserve and Nature Center. Across the parking lot, turn right at the nature center and follow signs to the Forest and Meadow Loop trails on the south side of the building.

1.0 Turn left on the Forest Loop Trail to follow the route clockwise.

1.2 Continue south onto the Meadow Loop Trail.

2.0 After returning to the Forest Loop Trail, continue north, heading toward the south side of the Boettcher Mansion and completing the nature preserve loop. Cross the road and retrace your steps back to the trailhead.

3.0 Arrive back at the Buffalo Bill Trailhead.

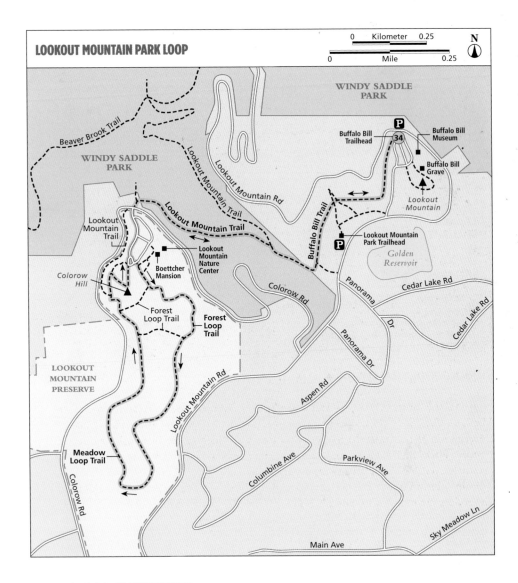

LOCAL INTEREST

Buffalo Bill's Pahaska Teepee Grille & Cafe: A charming eatery located inside the Buffalo Bill Museum gift shop, specializing in buffalo burgers and homemade fudge. 987 Lookout Mountain Rd., Golden; (303) 526-9367; buffalobill.org

LODGING

Table Mountain Inn: A Southwestern-themed property complete with an on-site Mexican restaurant in historic downtown Golden. 1310 Washington Ave., Golden; (303) 277-9898; tablemountaininn.com

35 CLEAR CREEK TRAIL— DOWNTOWN GOLDEN (PEAKS TO PLAINS TRAIL)

This short segment of the Clear Creek Trail passes right through downtown Golden, offering a quick sightseeing tour of some of the city's top attractions, and is often bustling with activity for premier people watching.

Elevation gain: 50 feet
Distance: 1.7-mile loop
Hiking time: About 20 minutes
Difficulty: Easy
Seasons: Year-round
Trail surface: Paved, dirt
Land status: City of Golden
Nearest town: Golden
Other trail users: Cyclists, joggers
Water availability: Yes, at trailhead

Canine compatibility: Yes, on leash
Fees and permits: None
Map: Regional Clear Creek Trail Map: cityofgolden.net/media/ClearCreekTrailMap.pdf
Trail contact: City of Golden Parks Department: (303) 384-8140
Trailhead GPS: N39 45.28' / E105 13.71'

FINDING THE TRAILHEAD

From downtown Denver, drive west on I-70 for about 9 miles. Take exit 265 onto SH-58 West toward Golden/Central City. In about 4.5 miles, exit onto Washington Avenue and turn left. In 3 blocks, turn right on 10th Street. Look for the parking lot on the left in 3 more blocks, on the southeast corner of Maple and 10th Streets across from Lions Park. (1201 10th Street, Golden)

WHAT TO SEE

Nestled at the base of Lookout Mountain underneath the striking rock face of North Table Mountain mesa, just 15 miles west of Denver, sits the city of Golden. Once the capital of the Colorado Territory following the 1850s gold rush, Golden is best known these days as home to the Coors Brewing Company and the Colorado School of Mines, as well as a charming downtown district that balances a collection of hip eateries and boutiques with historic Western character. This section of the Clear Creek Trail passes right through downtown, with easy access for a quick stroll to enjoy the beautiful foothills scenery and get a taste of what Golden has to offer.

Although this hike can be accessed by foot from anywhere in downtown Golden, the best place to park a car is at the Clear Creek Whitewater Park. Constructed from naturally occurring obstacles, this unique paddling course is divided into three sections offering 0.25 mile of fun and challenge for kayak, canoe, and SUP enthusiasts. The highly acclaimed design attracts a multitude of paddling events and competitions, providing entertainment for passersby year-round. Heading east on the paved path, you'll enjoy a view of the Golden Cliffs—a popular rock-climbing area of North Table Mountain. Although the creek is mesmerizing, don't forget to look up as you pass the Golden History Museum, or you'll miss a good photo opportunity in front of the cheerful *Greetings From Golden* outdoor mural.

This segment of the Clear Creek Trail meanders through downtown Golden and offers mountain views in every direction.

When you reach Washington Street, stay right to walk under the bridge, but take note of the Golden Visitor's Center on the corner. On the other side of the underpass you'll come face-to-face with a trio of bronze trout—one of many statues scattered along the trail. This one is titled *Return of the Cutthroat*, giving a nod to this section of water that is known for its optimal trout habitat, often referred to as the "Golden Mile" for fly-fishing. You'll also see a slide descending onto the trail from Parfet Park above and to the left. Here you'll follow the trail up a ramp (or take the stairs) and turn left, cutting through the park back toward the bridge you just walked under. Parfet Park offers a playground, parking area, restrooms, picnic tables, and ample grassy areas for resting in the shade. Perched on the banks of a mellow stretch of water, this is a popular place for people to sunbathe, wade and float in the river.

Take a left to cross over to the south side of the creek via the suspension bridge, lined with informational plaques depicting the city's heritage and round picnic tables overlooking the water. On the other side, look to your left for a glimpse of the Coors Brewing

The Clear Creek Whitewater Park offers a fun and challenging obstacle course for paddlers of all kinds, and entertainment for onlookers.

Parfet Park serves as the eastern border of this short loop, and is often crowded with people sunbathing, picnicking, and floating the river.

CLEAR CREEK TRAIL—DOWNTOWN GOLDEN (PEAKS TO PLAINS TRAIL)

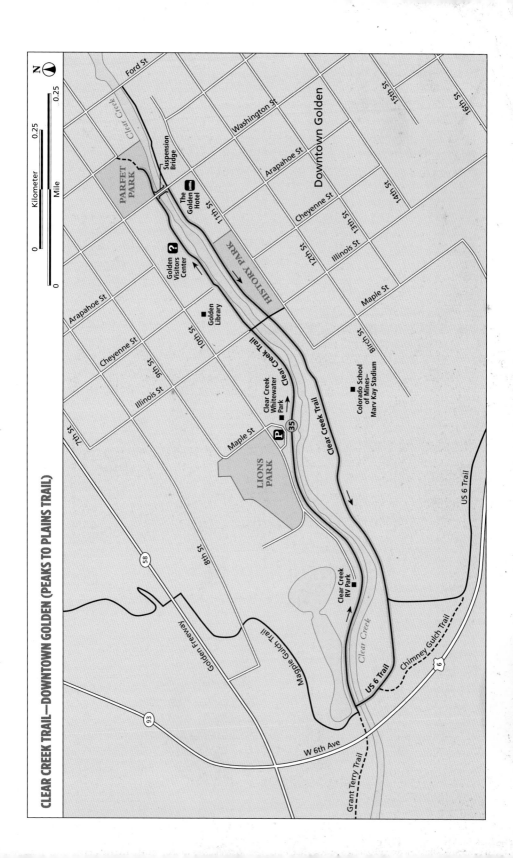

facility—the world's largest brewing operation, which is still producing its famous suds in the same location as its original establishment in 1873. Next, you'll turn right to head back toward to the trailhead along the south side of the creek. If you want to explore further, turn left instead, as the trail stretches eastward for about 4 miles until it connects with the Wheat Ridge Greenbelt trail. (The Clear Creek Trail is one of the main veins of the evolving Peaks to Plains Trail project, a 65-mile regional trail network that will ultimately connect downtown Denver to the Continental Divide at Loveland Pass. This guidebook features a few of the sections of trail that are already completed. See also the hike profiles for the Clear Creek Trail—Clear Creek Canyon segment in this section, and the Clear Creek Trail—Wheat Ridge Greenbelt section in the West Metro section.)

Just past the bridge, on the south side of the creek, you'll see the waterfront patio of the Bridgewater Grille at the Golden Hotel, a popular place for basking in the sun and enjoying the views with a cold beverage. The wrought-iron fence of the hotel patio quickly gives way to the split-rail fence of the Golden History Park, a historic homestead featuring a collection of restored ranch buildings including a blacksmith shop and schoolhouse, as well as a chicken coop and beehive. Continuing west, the sagebrush- and pine-dotted hillside of Lookout Mountain rises before you, creating a dramatic backdrop for the Colorado School of Mines athletic fields on the left (if you are here at dark you'll notice the glowing "M" built into the hillside, a student project that has since become incorporated into the school's legacy).

Soon after passing the school, the trail will turn north and cross the creek once again via a footbridge. After crossing, turn right and follow the path back to the trailhead parking lot.

MILES AND DIRECTIONS

0.0 Locate the trail south of the parking area, along the creek. Turn left to begin walking east, with the creek on your right-hand side.

0.17 Continue straight past the bridge.

0.35 Stay right toward the underpass.

0.46 Ascend the ramp or stairs on the left, toward Parfet Park. At the top, turn left to pass through the park toward the bridge.

0.53 Turn left to cross the bridge, then turn right on the paved path.

0.77 Continue straight, past the bridge.

1.2 Continue straight.

1.3 Continue straight, across the bridge, then turn right.

1.7 Arrive back at the trailhead/parking area.

LOCAL INTEREST

Golden City Brewing: Although there are many great craft breweries in Golden, this one stands out for its trail-focused beer names, like the Clear Creek Gold Kolsch and Lookout Mountain Stout, and because of its homegrown atmosphere—it is literally located in the owner's backyard. It also offers a rotating schedule of food trucks for sustenance. 920 12th St., Golden; (303) 279-8092; gcbrewery.com

Tributary Food Hall: Not sure what you have a hankering for, or traveling with a finicky group of varying tastes? Head to this delightful cafeteria-style bar and eatery where you can choose from a variety of vendors serving up everything from lattes and smoothie bowls to barbecue and street tacos, and plenty in between. 701 12th St., Golden; (303) 856-7225; tributarygolden.com

LODGING

The Golden Hotel: A classy-casual property in the heart of downtown featuring Western-themed artwork and a full-service restaurant and bar with a spacious patio overlooking the creek. 800 11th St., Golden; (303) 279-0100; thegoldenhotel.com

Golden Clear Creek RV Park: City owned and operated campsites just steps away from the creek and walking distance to downtown with full hookups, Wi-Fi, and laundry facilities. 1400 10th St., Golden; (303) 278-1437; cityofgolden.net/play/recreation-attractions/clear-creek-rv-park

36 PEAKS TO PLAINS TRAIL— CLEAR CREEK CANYON

Once an area reserved for experienced rock climbers, anglers, and kayakers, recent developments like a paved trail, hand railings, ample signage, and a paved parking lot with restrooms now make this canyon park accessible for all. Combined with a winding, scenic drive to the trailhead, this hike feels like a true mountain adventure.

Elevation gain: 271 feet
Distance: 7.8 miles out and back
Hiking time: About 3 hours
Difficulty: Moderate, due to elevation and length
Seasons: Year-round
Trail surface: Paved
Land status: Jefferson County Open Space, Clear Creek County
Nearest town: Golden
Other trail users: Cyclists, anglers, rock climbers, gold panning

Water availability: None
Canine compatibility: Yes, on leash
Fees and permits: None
Map: Jefferson County Clear Creek Canyon Park Map: jeffco.us/DocumentCenter/View/9365/Clear-Creek-Canyon-Park-Map
Trail contact: Jefferson County Open Space: (303) 271-5925
Trailhead GPS: N39 44.09' / W105 21.82'

FINDING THE TRAILHEAD

From downtown Denver, drive west on US 6 West for 14 miles. When you reach the city of Golden, turn left to stay on US 6 West/Clear Creek Canyon Road. The trailhead parking area will be on your left in 7 miles. (Clear Creek Canyon Big Easy Trailhead: 32088 US Hwy. 6, Golden)

WHAT TO SEE

In 2015 Colorado governor (now US senator) John Hickenlooper announced a plan to build a continuous trail from the city of Denver to the Continental Divide, connecting four counties, seven cities, and countless other existing trail networks along the way. The first segment of the 65-mile Peaks to Plains Trail was completed in 2017, giving pedestrians and cyclists the chance to get up close and personal with Clear Creek Canyon Park—a river and rock-climbing enthusiast's playground.

You'll start by walking east for a short time on a wide, concrete trail, passing by a well-developed picnic area featuring covered tables and a viewing platform along the water's edge. If it seems crowded, know that many visitors end their trek here, making quick use of the trailhead's restrooms and to snap a few photos of the creek before returning to their vehicles. You'll continue on, soon making your first pass over the creek via the Vasquez Bridge on your right (you'll be crossing the creek several times throughout the trek) before heading west to begin hiking in earnest.

Despite being carved alongside a mountain, the path is lined with willow and pine trees, providing some nice foliage and shade for a more varied landscape. Although you might catch a glimpse of bighorn sheep or foxes in the surrounding hills, the majority of the wildlife will be found on the water. In addition to the usual waterfowl like ducks

The vision of the Peaks to Plains Trail project is to make the mountains accessible for all.

and geese, watch for hawks and ospreys fishing for trout. Perhaps the most entertaining activity you'll see in the canyon is of the human sort—look for people scaling the rocky hills with ropes, fishing thigh-deep in the icy currents, and even panning for gold on the creek bank. Located just a few miles upstream, the tiny town of Idaho Springs was founded in 1859 as the state's first mining town and is known as the "home of the Colorado gold rush." Although it is illegal to remove natural resources from most open spaces in the county, prospecting is still a popular pastime for geology enthusiasts (also known as "rock hounds"), and you'll see signs indicating river access points around the Mayhem Gulch Trailhead.

After Mayhem Gulch—which also serves as a gateway to Centennial Cone Park, a popular trail system for hiking, mountain biking, and horseback riding—the next significant landmark you'll come to is the Cannonball Bridge. To be clear, the name is not due to this being a good place to do a cannonball jump into the water (quite the opposite!) but as a nod to the creek's original name of Cannonball Creek, due to the numerous boulders that fell into it. Notice the slight change of landscape after passing the Cannonball Flats Trailhead—here you'll see cactus and yucca plants on the hillside as you head northwest, and the trail starts to climb gradually uphill. If you're hiking in the winter, the trail might be more icy and snow-covered here, too.

The Placer Bridge takes you back to the non-highway side of the creek. Although the trail hugs the creek for its entirety, it also hugs the highway, which happens to be a popular trucking route. Admittedly, the traffic noise can be somewhat distracting at times, but it is a small price to pay for such lovely scenery.

winter walk presents wondrous frozen beauty.

Next you'll come to an underpass that marks the boundary for Clear Creek County. This final stretch is referred to as the "Oxbow" and is known for its rock-climbing crags. Here the trail carves briefly back to the east, away from the highway, making for a delightfully peaceful moment of silence and serenity. When you reach the Oxbow Trailhead, you'll turn around and make your way back to your starting point at the Big Easy Trailhead. While this is one of the longer trails featured in this book, don't expect to be bored on your return route. The changes of natural light over time in the canyon provide endless wonder and beauty, and you're likely to notice all kinds of things you didn't see before. Think of it this way—a long out and back doubles your chances of seeing wildlife! If you aren't enthused by this prospect, another option is to drive two cars and leave one at the Oxbow Trailhead to eliminate the return route, a tactic known as "shuttling."

MILES AND DIRECTIONS

0.0   Locate the trail on the southeast end of the parking area, beyond the restrooms.

0.15 Turn right to cross the creek via a footbridge.

0.19 Turn right, continuing west on the trail.

0.83 Continue straight, past the Mayhem Gulch Bridge.

1.6   Turn right, across the Cannonball Bridge.

2.0   Follow the trail across the Placer Bridge, continuing west.

2.8   Continue straight through the tunnel/underpass.

PEAKS TO PLAINS TRAIL—CLEAR CREEK CANYON

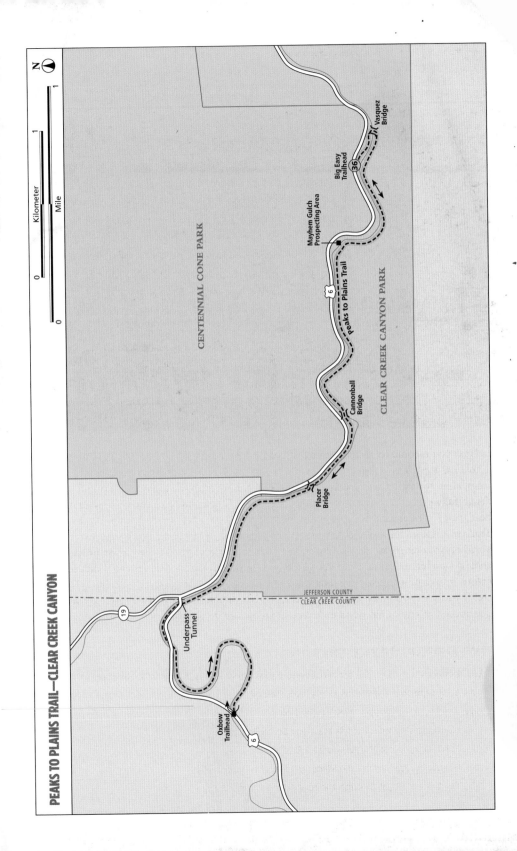

Rustic finishes on railings and signs help man-made features blend in nicely with natural ones.

3.9 Arrive at the Oxbow Trailhead. Turn around and retrace your steps back to the trailhead.

7.8 Arrive back at the Big Easy Trailhead and parking area.

LOCAL INTEREST

Beau Jo's Pizza: This famous Colorado institution is not to be confused with any ordinary pizza place—the pies are served by the pound, and its signature hand-rolled crust is served with a squeeze bottle of honey for drizzling, a unique technique that has become known as "Colorado-style." 1517 Miner St., Idaho Springs; (303) 567-4376; beaujos.com

Clear Creek Cidery & Eatery: Shake up your typical post-hike thirst-quencher with a visit to this "cidery" featuring a selection of some of the finest hard ciders around, as well as a hearty food menu with Southwestern flair. 1446 Miner St., Idaho Springs; (303) 567-2158; clearcreekcider.com

Phoenix Gold Mine: This award-winning attraction combines history and adventure into a 45-minute tour that starts with an informative look at an underground mine and ends with a hands-on gold panning lesson. 830 Trail Creek Rd., Idaho Springs; (303) 567-0422; phoenixgoldmine.com

LODGING

Indian Hot Springs Resort: A reservation at this vintage lodge includes passes to the on-site thermal pools, and few things feel better after a hike than a long, hot soak to soothe sore muscles. The property also features a variety of room types, including private cabins, which have hosted a slew of VIPs including Walt Whitman, Clint Eastwood, John Denver, and President Roosevelt. 302 Soda Creek Rd., Idaho Springs; (303) 989-6666; indianhotsprings.com

THE TEN ESSENTIALS OF HIKING

American Hiking Society

American Hiking Society recommends you pack the "Ten Essentials" every time you head out for a hike. Whether you plan to be gone for a couple of hours or several months, make sure to pack these items. Become familiar with these items and know how to use them. Learn more at **AmericanHiking.org/hiking-resources.**

 1. Appropriate Footwear

 6. Safety Items (light, fire, and a whistle)

 2. Navigation

 7. First Aid Kit

 3. Water (and a way to purify it)

 8. Knife or Multi-Tool

 4. Food

 9. Sun Protection

 5. Rain Gear & Dry-Fast Layers

 10. Shelter

PROTECT THE PLACES YOU LOVE TO HIKE

Become a member today and take $5 off
an annual membership using the code **Falcon5**.

AmericanHiking.org/join

American Hiking Society is the only national nonprofit
organization dedicated to empowering all to enjoy,
share, and preserve the hiking experience.

HIKE INDEX